DISCIPLES AND DEMOCRACY

MICHAEL CROMARTIE is a senior fellow and director of the Evangelical Studies Project at the Ethics and Public Policy Center in Washington, D.C. He is the co-editor, with Richard John Neuhaus, of *Piety and Politics: Evangelicals and Fundamentalists Confront the World*, and the editor of *Might and Right After the Cold War, No Longer Exiles: The Religious New Right in American Politics*, and other volumes.

DISCIPLES AND DEMOCRACY

Religious Conservatives and the Future of American Politics

Edited by
MICHAEL CROMARTIE

Foreword by
IRVING KRISTOL

ETHICS AND PUBLIC POLICY CENTER
WASHINGTON, D.C.

WILLIAM B. EERDMANS PUBLISHING COMPANY
GRAND RAPIDS, MICHIGAN

Copyright © 1994 by the Ethics and Public Policy Center
1015 Fifteenth St. N.W., Washington, D.C. 20005

Published jointly 1994 by the Ethics and Public Policy Center and
Wm. B. Eerdmans Publishing Co.
255 Jefferson Ave. S.E., Grand Rapids, Mich. 49503

Printed in the United States of America

Library of Congress Cataloging-in-Publication Data

Disciples and democracy: religious conservatives and the future of American politics /
edited by Michael Cromartie: foreword by Irving Kristol.
p.   cm.
Includes index.
ISBN 0-8028-0847-6
1. Evangelicalism—United States—History—20th century—Congresses.
2. Fundamentalism—History—Congresses. 3. Christianity and politics—History—
20th century—Congresses. 4. Conservatism—Religious aspects—Christianity—
History—20th century—Congresses. 5. Conservatism—United States—History—
20th century—Congresses. 6. United States—Politics and government—1989-1993—
Congresses. 7. United States—Politics and government—1993—Congresses.
8. United States—Church history—20th century—Congresses.
I. Cromartie, Michael.
BR1642.U5D57   1994
320.5'5'0973—dc20   94-21942
                                                                        CIP

Contents

FOREWORD

Taking Religious Conservatives Seriously

Irving Kristol

The beginning of political wisdom in the 1990s is the recognition that liberalism today is at the end of its intellectual tether. The fact that it can win elections is irrelevant. Conservatives continued to win elections during "the liberal century" (1870-1970), but once in office they were unable to enact a sustained conservative agenda. The tide of public opinion was too strong against them.

That tide has now turned. It is liberal administrations today, in all the Western democracies, that find themselves relatively impotent when in office. Just as conservative administrations used to nibble away at liberal reforms previously enacted, so liberals in office today do their share of nibbling at the occasional conservative reform that has taken hold. But more often, they find themselves nibbling away at the liberal reforms of their predecessors, reforms that threaten to bring about fiscal insolvency as well as political fragmentation.

The liberal consensus, as expressed in the media, is that, with the election of Bill Clinton, conservatism in America is in disarray, is groping for some center of equilibrium, and that only a "moderate" Republican coalition, one that disengages itself from the Religious Right, can create an American majority. This may be true in the shorter

---

Irving Kristol is editor of *The Public Interest* and publisher of *The National Interest*.

term, as defined by the next presidential election or two, but in the longer term it is false. The religious conservatives are already too numerous to be shunted aside, and their numbers are growing, as is their influence. They are going to be the very core of an emerging American conservatism.

For the past century the rise of liberalism has been wedded to the rise of secularism in all areas of American life. In the decades ahead, the decline of secularism will signify the decline of liberalism as well. Already, on the far-left fringes of liberalism itself, artists and philosophers are welcoming the collapse of a "secular humanism" that they find sterile and oppressive. They can offer nothing to replace this liberal-secular humanism. But others can, and will. Today, it is the religious who have a sense that the wave of the future is moving in their direction.

Three Pillars of Conservatism

The three pillars of modern conservatism are religion, nationalism, and economic growth. Of these, religion is easily the most important because it is the only power that, in the longer term, can shape people's characters and regulate motivation. In economics, secular incentives (i.e., materialist incentives) can be effective. But in the really troubled areas of modern life, where social policy is at work, the materialist incentives offered by the welfare state have given rise to a long train of calamities. Perverse economic incentives can encourage a corrupting dependency, and liberalism has, in the name of compassion, created a network of such perverse incentives.

But it does not follow that modifying these incentives will have a dramatic effect. The reason is simple: it is not possible to motivate people to do the right thing, and avoid doing the wrong thing, unless they are told, from childhood on, what the right things and the wrong things are. This explains why so many of our newer immigrants, coming from traditional families, are able to ignore these tempting, corrupting incentives and instead move on to productive and law-abiding lives.

The most extraordinary social phenomenon of the liberal century has been the totally unexpected increase in criminality. The first obligation of government has always been to ensure the security of the person. Liberalism does not believe this—it represents "too punitive" a conception of the governmental mission. Instead, liberalism believes that if you diminish income inequalities and provide cradle-to-grave income security and ample medical care, then the criminal impulse will wither away. In the face of increasing criminality, therefore, liberalism responds with ever more fanciful and ever more desperate "therapeutic" programs, all of which are ineffectual.

As with crime, so with all the other social pathologies that now infest our liberal society and its welfare state. "The joy of sex" has been compromised by an infusion of sexual anxiety, as venereal diseases ranging from the noxious to the fatal proliferate. It has also produced a large and growing population of unwed mothers and their babies. The liberal answer to this disaster is either to deny that it is any kind of disaster—"just a new kind of family," the social workers chirp—or to create more programs of "sex education." But such secular, non-judgmental education—an education bereft of moral guidance—has done much to create this problem in the first place.

Back in 1897, John Dewey defined the essence of the liberal credo: "The practical problem of modern society is the maintenance of the spiritual values of civilization, through the medium of the insight and decision of the individual." A noble idea but ultimately a self-contradictory one. You do not preserve spiritual values by turning them over to a rampant spiritual individualism. That experiment has been tried, and it has failed. But an admission of failure is not something we can expect. On the contrary: what we are witnessing is a prolonged spasm of liberal fanaticism—a redoubling of liberal effort as liberal program after liberal program fails. With each failure, the credibility of government is diminished and cynicism about politics increases. Does anyone really believe that the Clinton administration will significantly reduce, or that a second Bush administration would have significantly reduced, the budget deficit?

The plain truth is that if we are ever going to cope with the deficit, and the social programs that inflate it, we are going to have to begin with a very different view of human nature and human responsibility in relation to such issues as criminality, sexuality, welfare dependency, even medical insurance. Only to the degree that such a new—actually very old—way of looking at ourselves and our fellow citizens emerges can a public opinion be shaped that will candidly confront the fiscal crisis of the welfare state. Presidential calls for "sacrifice," meaning a willingness to pay higher taxes, are a liberal cop-out. Why don't we hear something about self-control and self-reliance? It's the traditional spiritual values that we as individuals need, not newly invented ones.

We hear it said frequently and with pseudo-solemnity that this fiscal crisis results from the people's demand for benefits that they are then unwilling to pay for. Were this so, the implication would be that these corrupt people are incapable of democratic self-government and need an elite to do the job for them. Liberals, despite their populist rhetoric, have been discreetly drawing this inference for many years now. Much of our overblown welfare state was created by liberal political entrepreneurs, not in response to an evident popular demand. Liberals may scornfully dismiss "supply-side" economics, but they are profoundly committed to "supply-side" politics—the politics of "unmet needs," a category that is constantly expanding. Also expanding, of course, are the official bureaucracies and the "helping" professions that cope with those "needs."

Reaffirming the Pillars

To counter the crisis that liberalism is provoking in our society, conservatism has to rediscover and reaffirm its attachment to its three traditional pillars of religion, nationalism, and economic growth. A reaffirmation of the goal of economic growth should not be difficult. It is becoming ever more widely appreciated that economic growth is crucially dependent on the ability of "economic activists" to invest and innovate. Just as political activists, spurred by political ambition, are at the heart of liberal public policy, so economic activists, spurred by economic ambition, are at the heart of conservative economic policy. It is they who promote the growth that pacifies egalitarian and redistributional appetites. There is still an influential segment of "old conservatives" who do not understand that a pro-entrepreneurial emphasis in economic policy is not simply a "pro-business" policy. But they are gradually fading away.

Similarly, an affirmation of the national spirit is practically inevitable, as the liberal internationalism that has defined American foreign policy since the days of Woodrow Wilson continues to unravel. The United States will surely want to, and will need to, remain an active world power, but this activity will not be within the confines prescribed by the United Nations or NATO or whatever. In this post-

Cold War era, those organizations are on their way to becoming moribund. Nor are we about to engage in some kind of benign humanitarian imperialism—except in very special circumstances, decided case by case. A renascent nationalism will be accompanied by a renascent neo-realism in foreign policy. This is something that most conservatives have long wished for.

Coping with a religious revival, however, is something that conservatives and the Republican Party are not yet prepared for, and that the Democrats seem almost entirely uninterested in. Religious people always create problems, since their ardor tends to outrun the limits of politics in a constitutional democracy. But if American public life is to retain some semblance of civility, we had all better work hard at understanding these people.

This book can help us do that. The commentators offer a wealth of information on religious conservatives: what they want, how they affected the last presidential election, what political influence they are likely to have in the years ahead, and how they can most effectively present their views in a pluralistic society.

In a sense, the influx of the religious conservatives into American politics is analogous to the influx of European immigrants into our urban centers between 1870 and 1914. Although the immigrants created many problems, the Democrats welcomed them while the Republicans shunned them. That was the origin of the "natural" Democratic majority. But the Democrats are very unlikely to welcome the religious conservatives in the foreseeable future. If the Republicans, too, keep them at arm's length instead of embracing them and shaping their political thinking, a third party and a restructuring of American politics are certain. One way or another, in the decades ahead they will not be denied.

Adapted from the February 1, 1993, issue of the *Wall Street Journal* by permission of the author.

Preface

All political communities, said Saint Augustine, even the very best, are analogous to "bands of robbers." It is a point with which many leaders of the Religious Right would heartily agree. But many other Americans fear the political activism of these evangelical and fundamentalist Christians, because they seem to want to replace the current "bands of robbers" with their own bands of believers. This is not a comfortable prospect for people who disagree with their policy prescriptions.

In a now notorious front-page story in 1993, a reporter for the *Washington Post* characterized members of the Religious Right as "largely poor, uneducated, and easy to command." The description recalls H. L. Mencken's sneering comments on the Religious Right of his day. In his dispatches from the Scopes Trial in Dayton, Tennessee, in 1925, Mencken described evangelicals and fundamentalists as "halfwits," "yokels," "rustic ignoramuses," "anthropoid rabble," and "gaping primates of the upland valleys" who subscribe to a "childish theology."

To the distress of their opponents and to the delight of their political allies, the "gaping primates of the upland valleys" are still very much with us and have become a large voting bloc. And they are largely neither uneducated, nor poor, nor easy to command. Despite their disillusionment with some aspects of the Reagan presidency, despite their grave disappointment with the Bush administration, and despite their distress over the election of Bill Clinton, they remain as determined as ever to make their voice heard in a society that seems to have lost its moral moorings. Many have learned the truth of the definition of politics as "the art of the possible"—the art, in Reinhold Niebuhr's phrase, of "finding approximate solutions to basically insoluble problems." It sometimes requires prudent and principled compromise. "Politics," said Max Weber, "is the slow boring of hard surfaces."

In December 1993 the Ethics and Public Policy Center brought together a diverse group of twenty-eight scholars, activists, and journalists to assess the impact of the Religious Right on the Bush-Clinton presidential contest of 1992 and to explore the future prospects for conservative Christian political action. The conference, entitled "The Religious New Right: The 1992 Campaign and Beyond," was sponsored by the Center's Evangelical Studies Project. For a day and a half the participants engaged in a lively and stimulating exchange centered on papers presented by Ralph Reed, executive director of the Christian Coalition, John Green, political science professor at the University of Akron, and George Weigel, president of the Ethics and Public Policy Center. Each of the three papers was followed by responses from two distinguished commentators. This volume also includes pertinent comments made by various other participants (identified on pages 117-18) in response to the presentations.

Ralph Reed speculates on what American society would look like if the Religious Right were successful. Religious conservatives seeking to "redress the social chaos of the last quarter century" have often had "their motives impugned" and "their agenda caricatured." Reed insists that religious conservatives are not attempting to establish a theocracy or to break down the separation of church and state. They "should be welcomed in the public square," he says, "not greeted with fear."

John Green and his colleagues analyze voting data from the 1992 presidential campaign and conclude that religious conservatives did not play "the pernicious role in Bush's defeat commonly assigned to them." (Green presented the paper at the conference, which is why comments on it refer to him alone.) Polling data indicate that, on balance, Bush gained votes by his social-issue conservatism; however, these gains were offset by negative responses to the administration's economic performance. Green and his colleagues conclude that "evangelicals are now an important Republican voting bloc, social-issue conservatism represents a source of Republican votes, and the Christian Right appears to be a modestly helpful ally."

George Weigel argues that religious conservatives must develop a more disciplined public discourse, an ecumenical "grammar" by which they can effectively advance their views in the public arena. He maintains that a new appreciation of natural-law theory is urgently needed because that theory represents, "even under the conditions of the Fall, a moral logic built into the world and into us, a logic that reasonable men and women can grasp by disciplined reflection on the dynamics of human action."

In an afterword, journalist Fred Barnes challenges widespread myths about the Religious Right that are prevalent in the media. He also underscores their critical political and moral role in current public-policy debates. Religious conservatives keep many issues of urgent concern "on the table" for debate, he says.

As is apparent from this brief overview, "Religious Right" is not a unanimously accepted term for the part of the population we are examining. Some contributers to this volume use it; others use, instead, "Christian Right," or "religious conservatives," or "evangelicals" (which, incidentally, is capitalized in chapter two of this book, where it refers to a voting bloc, but not elsewhere).

I would like to thank several colleagues at the Ethics and Public Policy Center. Senior editor Carol Griffith, with her usual consummate skill, edited the conference materials for this book. Eric Owens helped organize the conference and did heroic work in transcribing tapes and typing the manuscript. Marianne Geers provided timely and always cheerful assistance.

Since the late nineteenth century, observes historian Grant Wacker, evangelicals "have always known how to play political hardball when the prayer meeting let out." Although some political observers felt that the election of Bill Clinton signaled the end of the Religious Right's influence in American politics, that influence appears to be waxing rather than waning. We hope this book will encourage constructive and critical thinking inside and outside the evangelical community on how religious conservatives can most effectively incorporate moral values derived from Christian conviction into political decision-making.

MICHAEL CROMARTIE

1

What Do Religious Conservatives Really Want?

Ralph E. Reed, Jr.

During the 1960 presidential campaign John F. Kennedy was often questioned about his Catholic faith and whether it would negatively affect his service as the nation's president. He would reply, "No one asked about my religion when I served my country in the South Pacific, or when my brother gave his life for his country over the English Channel." Today, the finger of suspicion is again pointed at people of faith. This time the target is not, as in the past, Jews or Catholics, but rather evangelical Protestants. Some have called into question the right of evangelicals to participate fully in American public life. Their motives have been impugned, their agenda caricatured, with the implication that their religious beliefs disqualify them from public service.

An editorial in the *New York Times* warned that the political activism of religious conservatives "poses a far greater threat to democracy than was presented by Communism."[1] Columnist Molly Ivins has suggested revoking the tax-exempt status of churches unless they "shut their holy yaps" about controversial issues like abortion and pornog-

Ralph E. Reed, Jr., is executive director of the Christian Coalition, the nation's largest pro-family organization, with a million members and activists in all fifty states. Its headquarters are in Chesapeake, Virginia.

raphy.[2] When a respected female churchgoer and businesswoman announced her candidacy for the U.S. Senate in Nebraska in 1993, the state Democratic Party chairman launched a verbal attack on her, labeling her a "Christian Coalition type." At about the same time, voters in Virginia witnessed a vicious and bigoted campaign against Michael Farris, the Republican nominee for lieutenant governor, that was largely based on falsehoods about Farris's litigation in a school textbook case in Tennessee.[3]

Imagine the outrage the cultural elite would express if someone referred to a Jewish candidate as a "B'nai B'rith type." They would rightly condemn such prejudice. Yet bigoted assaults of this sort are frequently visited upon Christian candidates for public office. This kind of bigotry was wrong when it was directed at Jews, Catholics, and others in the past. It is wrong when it is directed at evangelical Protestants today.

No one asked my father's religion before sending him to serve on an aircraft carrier in Vietnam. No one asked Pat Robertson his religion when he served his country with distinction as a U.S. Marine in Korea. No one asked Oliver North his religion when he served in Vietnam, earning two Purple Hearts and a Distinguished Service Cross. If their religion did not disqualify them on the battlefield or the high seas, then it certainly should not keep them out of the public square.

In the United States today, one out of every three births occurs out of wedlock, one out of two marriages ends in divorce, one out of three pregnancies ends in abortion, and inner-city males 18 to 35 have a higher likelihood of being killed than an American soldier had in Vietnam. Despite this flood of violence and social chaos, there are still some who believe that the most dangerous thing that could possibly happen in this country would be for religious conservatives to become active in government.

A brief word about terms: I do not use "the Religious Right" as a term of self-identification. First, it is badly out of date, since it refers to a movement that flowered in the late 1970s as part of the New Right. Second, it has become a pejorative term that connotes an intolerant and extremist political agenda. No one refers to the National Council of Churches or the Southern Christian Leadership Conference as "the Religious Left." I prefer "religious conservative" and "pro-family conservative" and will use these terms interchangeably.

Envisioning the Changes

What would the world look like if religious conservatives won? Not, as some might have us believe, like the Soviet Union under the second Five Year Plan or Germany during the Third Reich. Compared to other social movements, religious conservatives have espoused a public-policy agenda that is quite mainstream and non-threatening. The Populists of the 1880s and 1890s wanted to take the money supply off the gold standard, nationalize the railroads, and provide credit to farmers through a revolutionary sub-treasury plan in which the value of crops put in storage would be used to back federal currency. These were radical measures, proposed in an apocalyptic and even paranoid rhetorical style. The Progressive movement during the early part of this century called for a steeply progressive income tax, anti-trust legislation, and the creation of the Federal Reserve System. Some modern social movements such as feminism and the New Left have called for radical social change and for revolutionary government policies.

The agenda of religious conservatives is, by contrast, quite unremarkable. What most religious conservatives really want is to reclaim some strengths of the America that most of us grew up in, the post–World War II America that was proud, militarily strong, morally sound, and looked up to by the rest of the world. This America existed until the nation's cultural fabric was torn apart by a combination of the sexual revolution, the war in Vietnam, Watergate, the rise of the drug culture, and the explosive growth of the welfare state.

The America envisioned by religious conservatives, then, encompasses much of what was good about America for most of the history of the republic and adds to this some more recent gains. As the foundation: marriages that work and a far greater proportion of intact, two-parent families. Lower taxes, less bureaucracy, leaner government. A thriving, expanding economy with less job-killing government regulation. An educational system without rival. Greater empowerment of private citizens to free themselves from dependency on government programs. Hard-core and child pornography illegal and socially stigmatized. Abortion rare and largely restricted to the hard cases of rape, incest, or endangerment of the mother's life. Voluntary, student-initiated school prayer and other public expressions of faith protected as free speech under the First Amendment. Television shows and movies that celebrate the family and elevate the human spirit and do not glorify violence, extramarital sex, vulgar language, and human cruelty. A color-blind society in which people are judged by their abilities rather than by their skin color, gender, or national origin. A tougher criminal-justice system that puts violent offenders behind bars, while providing rehabilitative alternatives to incarceration for young, non-violent offenders.

Religious conservatives want to move forward, not backward. Many of the social changes of the past thirty years are advances that must be preserved. For example, the movement of women in the workplace to a position of equality where they can advance as far as their talents can carry them is clearly progress, as are the achievements of the civil-rights movement in bringing minorities closer to full equality. But the policy failures and cultural excesses that have led to our current rates of illegitimacy, divorce, drug use, abortion, violent crime, pornography, and illiteracy must be corrected.

The Social Pathologies

While the population has risen 41 per cent since 1960, violent crime has risen 560 per cent. There were 4.7 million crimes in 1964 and 14.8 million in 1990.[4] The problem is exacerbated by a liberal and lenient criminal-justice system and by overcrowded prisons, resulting in the premature release of hardened criminals. The person arrested for the abduction and murder of a twelve-year-old girl in California in late 1993 was a career criminal and vagrant who was out on parole after serving only five years of a fifteen-year sentence for a previous kidnapping.

Nearly a third of all criminals convicted of a felony serve *no time* in prison. For murderers in the United States, the median sentence served is six years; for rapists, three years; for drug dealers, one year. Of the more than 13 million arrests by local law enforcement annually, less than 2 per cent result in a prison sentence. According to the National Center for Policy Analysis, there are approximately 6 million burglaries in America every year, but only 72,000 burglars go to prison —an incarceration rate of barely 1 per cent.[5]

Education is in a state of crisis. In 1960, we spent $2,035 per pupil on education (in constant 1990 dollars). Today per-pupil spending has more than doubled, to $5,247, but SAT scores have declined all but one year since 1960. One recent study found that two-thirds of high school seniors could not identify the decade in which the Civil War was fought. American schoolchildren trail their counterparts in every major industrialized nation in the world in math, science, history, and geography test scores.

The rates of divorce and out-of-wedlock births have spiraled to unprecedented levels. As Daniel Patrick Moynihan argued in 1965, "there is one unmistakable lesson in American history: a community that allows a large number of young men to grow up in broken families asks for and gets chaos." In such a society, "crime, violence, unrest, unrestrained lashing out at the whole social structure—that is not only to be expected, it is very near inevitable."[6] When Moynihan wrote these words, the illegitimacy rate for black babies was 22 per cent. That rate has now been reached by white babies, while the out-of-wedlock rate for black babies has risen to 68 per cent.

Marriage has fared no better since 1960. In that year there were only 393,000 divorces, and three out of four marriages stayed intact. By 1992 the number of divorces had risen to 1.2 million. According to the University of Wisconsin's National Survey of Families and Households, six out of every ten new marriages will fail. Each year one million children are victims of divorce. According to the U.S. Census Bureau, 60 per cent of all children in the United States will lose a parent to divorce before they reach the age of 18.

The emotional and psychological cost is enormous. "There is a mountain of scientific evidence showing that when families disintegrate, children often end up with intellectual, physical, and emotional scars that persist for life," argues social scientist Karl Zinsmeister. "We talk about the drug crisis, the education crisis, and the problems of teen pregnancy and juvenile crime, but all of these ills trace back predominantly to one source: broken families."[7]

Why the sudden rise in these social pathologies beginning in the mid-1960s? The causal connection is not altogether clear. Some social commentators like Charles Murray have pointed to a revolution in social policy associated with the Great Society. Others blame the sexual revolution and the feminist movement. William Raspberry suggests, with particular regard to the African-American family, that the root cause is the disintegration of a sense of community. Strong institutions of enculturation—churches, parochial schools, neighborhood associations, black colleges—decayed or lost their influence. No doubt all these factors played a role. But there can also be no doubt that there is a correlation between a decline in the role of religion in our society and the rise of social pathologies of every kind. The Supreme Court decisions outlawing voluntary prayer in schools, aid to parochial schools, and public display of the Ten Commandments were signposts along the road to a declining role of religion and faith in American culture. The 1960s and 1970s were decades in which faith and religious institutions lost much of their influence, and in which government policy became biased against the valuable social role religion plays in stabilizing marriages, nurturing young people, and knitting together communities.

Liberals and conservatives alike are now acknowledging that our society has become too militantly secular, our public discourse too coarse and vulgar, and our culture too hostile to religious values. "We err when we presume that religious motives are likely to be illiberal," argues Stephen L. Carter in *The Culture of Disbelief,* "and we compound the error when we insist that the devout should keep their religious ideas—whether good or bad—to themselves."[8]

Causes of Contempt

If society is plagued by serious social problems—crime, illegitimacy, illiteracy, family breakup—and if religious conservatives advocate solutions that are supported by millions of people, why are pro-family conservatives so often portrayed as zealots whose agenda is, *ipso facto,* undemocratic?

Part of the blame is our own. William Rusher once observed that the only difference between Barry Goldwater and Ronald Reagan was that Goldwater spoke with a scowl while Reagan spoke with a smile. Sometimes the *manner* in which something is said is more important than what is actually said. The devout have too often spoken in the public square with a scowl or in a way that shut out or offended some of their listeners. A former president of the Southern Baptist Convention asserted publicly in 1980 that "God does not hear the prayers of Jews." In 1992, a group of Christian leaders distributed a pamphlet that trumpeted the warning: "To vote for Bill Clinton is a sin against God." These statements presented a harsh side of religious belief that is simply inappropriate in a political context.

But religious conservatives have not brought all their problems of image on themselves. Equally to blame are the media, which inadequately cover the positive and affirming side of religious faith, and tend to report only activities and statements that reinforce a negative stereotype. A prime example was the infamous description of evangelicals by Michael Weisskopf in a front-page story in the *Washington Post:* "poor, uneducated, and easy to command."[9] To the extent that religious leaders and organizations take stands consistent with the prevailing "politically correct" agenda, their moral statements may be welcomed, not condemned. When Martin Luther King, Jr., in his "Letter from Birmingham Jail," proclaimed that "just law is a man-made code that squares with the moral law or the law of God," no one objected to his introduction of religion into a public-policy issue. But similar references to God's law made by conservative religious leaders in connection with such causes as opposition to abortion are likely to elicit hysterical cries that they threaten the "separation of church and state."

Family-Friendly Policy

Religious conservatives believe that the first principle of public policy with regard to the family should be, "Do no harm." This principle, though it may seem unexceptionable, has been violated repeatedly by Washington during the past three decades. While recognizing that government cannot guarantee that families stay together, religious conservatives want government to be family-friendly, to stop penalizing two-parent, working families while subsidizing family breakup. Take tax policy: In 1950, the average family of four paid just 2 per cent of its adjusted gross income in federal income taxes. Today that figure is 24 per cent. When state income taxes, sales taxes, property taxes, and local fees are added in, the average family of four spends 37 per cent of its income on taxes—more than it spends on food (10 per cent), housing (20 per cent), and clothing (2-5 per cent), combined. Pro-family conservatives have made a dramatic increase in the standard tax deduction for children one of their priorities. If the personal exemption had kept pace with inflation since World War II, today it would be approximately $8,300 instead of $2,300. No family of four in America making less than $33,000 a year would pay a dime in federal income tax.

Tax policy should reflect two family-friendly principles. First, income dedicated to providing for the basic needs of children—food, clothing, housing, health care, and education—should be exempt from taxation. The family is the most efficient and effective Department of Health, Education, and Welfare ever conceived. It is far more efficient to leave dollars devoted to basic needs in the family budget than to confiscate them through the tax code and then filter them back through the federal bureaucracy. A second principle is that income dedicated to creating jobs should be exempt from taxation. Job creation, particularly in areas with high unemployment and a high incidence of family breakup, should be at the top of any family-friendly economic agenda. The government should encourage the job-creating capacity of the economy by lowering the capital-gains tax, creating urban enterprise zones in depressed areas, and reducing taxes and regulations on small business.

Limiting Government

Regarding the first principle: doubling the standard deduction for children would cost approximately $132 billion over five years. Large though that figure is, it is far less than the cost of providing for children through a government bureaucracy. But to compensate for the decreased revenue, the federal budget must be put on a diet.

Religious conservatives support a balanced-budget amendment to the Constitution that would limit taxation to a reasonable percentage of the Gross Domestic Product (somewhere around 20 per cent) and require Congress to spend no more than available revenues. We are in favor of requiring a supermajority in both houses of Congress, similar to that required to invoke cloture in the Senate, to pass any tax increase.

A line-item veto, already given to forty-three state governors, should be granted to the nation's president. Entitlement spending should be controlled by means-testing, limiting spending growth to the increase in inflation and population, and requiring larger contributions from those most able to pay. In addition, we favor the kinds of spending cuts advocated by Congressmen John Kasich and Tim Penny: reducing the federal work force by 252,000 jobs, requiring larger co-payments from well-to-do Medicare recipients, and eliminating regional offices of Housing and Urban Development and the Department of Agriculture.

The founding fathers envisioned the United States Congress as a citizen legislature. In the *Federalist Papers,* Alexander Hamilton predicted that the frequency of elections for the House of Representatives would ensure a high turnover in membership and would guarantee a close relationship between Congress and the people. But with the reelection rate for incumbents now around 90 per cent, Congress bears little resemblance to that vision today. Religious conservatives favor limiting terms, and applying to former members of Congress the same limits on post-service lobbying that apply to the executive branch. Congressional reform is an important component of a broader vision of religious conservatives: to limit government by diminishing the control of career politicians and bureaucrats and restoring an ethic of government service by average citizens.

Reforming Welfare, Reducing Crime

While the tax code penalizes working families, the welfare system subsidizes family breakup. The government subsidizes people if they exhibit three patterns of behavior: they must not work, they must not stay married, and they must bear children out of wedlock. Not surprisingly, all three of these social pathologies have skyrocketed over the past thirty years. The cost of Aid to Families with Dependent Children (AFDC) alone has risen from $3.6 billion in 1970 to $22.4 billion in 1993, while we spend approximately $308 billion on all welfare programs. During the same period the number of families on welfare has risen from 1.9 million to 4.7 million. Of all children born in 1980, 22 per cent of white children and 83 per cent of black children will be on welfare before they reach age 18.

President Clinton is promising to end welfare as we know it, but at greater cost. The White House has proposed giving a $5,000 grant to any private employer who hires a welfare recipient. The assumption is that the main problem facing welfare recipients is lack of employment opportunities. The Clinton welfare strategy is flawed precisely because it fails to address the root cause of government dependency: family breakup and illegitimacy. This is not, as some might have us believe, a "Murphy Brown" syndrome: only 6 per cent of women above the poverty line bear children out of wedlock, while 44 per cent of women below the poverty line do so. Illegitimacy is a life sentence to poverty for millions of children.

Charles Murray's 1993 essay on the white underclass stimulated the greatest debate over welfare reform since the late 1960s.[10] Murray proposed that we cut illegitimacy by (1) removing the economic subsidy (that is, AFDC payments) and (2) regenerating the social stigma associated with out-of-wedlock births. He thinks this would deter many from joining the ranks of those who bring children into the world without the means to provide for them.

If that is the "stick," then perhaps a "carrot" would be to eliminate the marriage penalty under the current welfare system by providing slightly higher subsidies for poor women who bear children within marriage. Or, the earned-income tax credit could be expanded for children in two-parent households. Another important goal should be eliminating the vast welfare bureaucracy and getting the aid directly to the families that need it, again with a bias towards marriage and intact families. Total welfare spending at all levels of government for an eligible family of four, a figure that now totals over $32,000, is higher than the median income for families. Clearly, welfare spending is not getting to lower-income families as efficiently as it should.

The federal government should lift all restrictions on state experimentation in welfare reform. Beyond this, some reforms that have already proven successful at the state level should be enacted. First, workfare requirements should be mandatory for all able-bodied males and all females whose children are above pre-school age. Around half of the single mothers on welfare do not have children under age five. The same requirement should apply to food-stamp recipients. Second, the establishment of paternity should be required for children receiving welfare or food stamps. Current law requires that mothers make a "good faith" effort to establish paternity. This law is often ignored. Men who are identified as fathers should be required to provide child-support payments to defray welfare costs. Local experiments in Wisconsin with the establishment of paternity and requirements for child support have resulted in dramatic reductions in AFDC caseloads in some locales. The policy rationale is that any man responsible for bringing a child into the world should be primarily responsible for supporting that child.[11]

We must also provide greater stability for the most important contract in civilized society: the marriage contract. Even in the absence of an economic incentive for illegitimacy, we cannot ultimately make progress on social problems like crime, poverty, illiteracy, and drug abuse without saving marriages. We should reconsider "no fault" divorce laws that allow men to marry women and father children, only to abandon them for any reason or no reason at all. The average divorced woman's income declines 70 per cent during the first year following divorce. The economic inviability of single motherhood has long been established. There should be social and legal sanctions against men who shirk their responsibilities to wives and children, and divorce laws should encourage marriages to stay together rather than break apart.

Crime is another problem that will defy solution until we deal with the root causes of family breakup. As George Gilder has observed, single men compose only 13 per cent of the population, yet they make up 40 per cent of prison inmates, and commit 90 per cent of violent crimes. Single men disconnected from the social responsibilities of families are, statistically speaking, more inclined to lash out violently at the social order.[12] Children raised in homes without fathers are twice as likely to commit crime, three times as likely to drop out of high school, and twice as likely to become dependent upon drugs or alcohol. One useful step in decreasing crime is alternative sentencing to boot camps and halfway houses for youthful, first-time offenders. An experiment under way in the District of Columbia assigns a non-violent offender to a church and a family in the community that report to the criminal-justice system on the young offender's progress. Parole should be eliminated for violent criminals. Restitution programs should allow payment of debts directly to victims rather than to society at large.

Protecting the Unborn

Religious conservatives believe that government should protect innocent human life. The inalienable right to life is affirmed in our Declaration of Independence, was recognized in our laws for three centuries, and is codified in the Fourteenth Amendment to the Constitution. *Roe* v. *Wade* was a disastrous decision that imposed the liberal abortion laws of two states, New York and Colorado, upon the rest of the nation. It was one of the most ill-conceived acts of judicial fiat since the *Dred Scott* decision, and it has created no less civil discord. Liberals treat *Roe* as, according to Abraham Lincoln, Stephen Douglas treated *Dred Scott:* as a "thus saith the Lord." Religious conservatives want to return this issue to the legislative arena, where it belongs, and allow state legislatures to enact commonsense restrictions on abortion, such as waiting periods and the requiring of parental consent when the girl is a minor. Should a state seek to restrict abortion to cases of rape, incest, and endangerment of the mother's life, it should not be prevented from doing so.

Lincoln said, "We shall not have peace until . . . the opponents of slavery will arrest the further spread of it, and place it where the public mind shall rest in the belief that its course is of ultimate extinction." His vision was to promote the withering away of a vast social evil by cutting off its source (the slave trade) and stemming its spread (to the territories). Religious conservatives have the same vision for abortion. They seek to stop taxpayer subsidies—direct and indirect—to organizations that promote or perform abortions, and to stop the spread of abortion by allowing states to impose reasonable restrictions on it. The American people agree. According to a recent Gallup poll, 72 per cent of the American people oppose taxpayer subsidies for elective abortions.

In addition, we must encourage adoption as a matter of public policy. Our goal should be to provide loving homes for children born out of wedlock, rather than shuttling them from one foster-care arrangement to the next. There are only 370,000 children in foster care, while there are more than a million couples seeking to adopt. Because so few babies are available for adoption, and because of the innumerable legal obstacles to adoption, a system of private adoption agencies and "surrogate mothers" has sprung up. Adoption laws should be reformed to promote rather than discourage adoption: for instance, regulations prohibiting interracial adoption and imposing strict age limits on prospective parents should be relaxed.

Reforming Education

Educational reform is one of the most important items on the agenda of religious conservatives. They favor replacing the vast educational bureaucracy with a system that empowers parents and teachers. School choice is an idea whose time has come. Although defeated in California in 1993, it will almost certainly appear on other state ballots in the years to come, with greater success. Surveys show that 70 per cent of the American people believe parents should be able to choose the best school for their children, whether private, public, or parochial. Post-election polls conducted in California indicated that Proposition 174, the school-choice initiative, would have passed if the proponents had established clearer guidelines for voucher schools and if the students currently enrolled in private schools had been grandfathered into the scholarship program, insuring no reduction in per-pupil spending in the public schools.

Even if school choice succeeds, the vast majority of students, probably 70-80 per cent, will remain in public schools. The public-education agenda of religious conservatives is simple. First, empower local teachers by cutting state and federal bureaucracy and mandates. Second, implement a back-to-basics curriculum with an emphasis on basic reading and math skills, backed up by standards for promotion and regular testing. Third, establish merit pay and performance standards for teachers to encourage the best and brightest to enter the profession. Fourth, require that schools encourage young people to postpone sexual activity until marriage. Experimental abstinence-based programs like Sex Respect and Teen Aid have reduced the incidence of teen pregnancy, abortion, and drug use by as much as 50 per cent in some school districts.

Educational reform must also address what William Bennett has called the "architecture of the soul." Children should be taught to distinguish right from wrong. They are moral creatures and should be treated as such. Likewise, they should not be prohibited from exercising their right to free speech, including speech with religious content.

On this point, the government and courts have failed our children badly. The "Lemon test," derived from the 1971 Supreme Court decision Lemon v. Kurtzman, requires that to be constitutional a school statute must meet three criteria: it must have a primary secular purpose, it must neither advance nor inhibit religion, and it must not promote excessive entanglement of government with religion. In some cases, the effort to monitor or regulate speech or activity so that it meets the second Lemon requirement has in itself been judged to constitute "excessive entanglement" and thus to violate the third requirement. Any kind of prayer—no matter how non-sectarian—at graduation ceremonies has been prohibited.

The consequences have been dismaying. The Supreme Court struck down a law that allowed for the teaching of scientific creationism in tandem with evolution on the curious grounds that most supporters of the law were religious. In the fall of 1993, 280 students were suspended from a high school in Mississippi after they refused to abide by the school district's policy banning the recitation of a simple prayer composed by students and read at the start of the day over the school intercom. A majority of the students in this predominantly black high school voted for the prayer, which read: "Almighty God, we ask that you bless our parents, teachers and country throughout the day. In your name we pray, Amen." Only a last-minute reinstatement of the suspended students by school officials averted a statewide walkout by students protesting this act of censorship. The time has come for the courts to allow free speech—including non-sectarian, student-initiated prayer—in public schools.[13]

A Culture of Caring

This is the agenda of the pro-family movement: family-friendly tax and welfare policy, commonsense limits on government, schools that work, the right of parents to protect their children from instruction or practices that they consider immoral or anti-religious, and safe neighborhoods. It is an agenda that recognizes the limits of what public policy can achieve, yet demands that government restore the centrality of the two-parent family in the social structure that this policy promotes. It is an agenda that seeks to encourage what is normal, and discourage what is deviant, i.e., crime, illegitimacy, divorce, illiteracy, poverty, and drug abuse. As Charles Krauthammer notes, this posits a role for government that was taken for granted thirty years ago but signals a real departure today. "The real deviants of society stand unmasked," writes Krauthammer. "Who are they? Not Bonnie and Clyde, but Ozzie and Harriet."[14]

Religious conservatives envisage a larger role for private philanthropy and religious institutions in creating a culture of caring. Homes for unwed mothers, halfway houses for troubled teens, parochial schools, and congregate care centers to replace the foster-home system are all part of a nurturing network that religious conservatives hope to erect. Churches must do more than send newlyweds down the aisle and out the door: they must also provide instruction and counseling to help mend broken marriages and heal hurting families. Literacy programs in the inner city and rural areas must teach people how to read and write when the schools fail to do so. Alternative schools must be available as the first rung on the ladder out of the ghetto for inner-city youth whose public schools are all too often war zones.

There are encouraging signs that the public is ready to give people of faith a role in government. In July 1993 the people of Arkansas elected Mike Huckabee, a Baptist minister and former president of the Arkansas Baptist Convention, as the first Republican lieutenant governor in that state in 130 years. And Michael Farris received 47 per cent of the vote in his campaign for lieutenant governor in Virginia that year, despite being outspent considerably on television by a well-entrenched incumbent. Farris got more votes than Mary Sue Terry, the Democratic nominee for governor. In a historic turnout, persons who identified themselves as born-again evangelicals totaled 38 per cent of the voting electorate. When voters were asked whether the attacks on Farris's religious beliefs made them want to vote Republican or Democrat, 17 per cent said Republican, 9 per cent said Democrat, and 70 per cent said the attacks made no difference. These survey results suggest that attacks on religion do not have the desired result at the polls and may actually result in a net gain for Republican candidates.[15]

"Despotism may be able to do without religion," observed Alexis de Tocqueville in 1835, "but democracy most assuredly cannot." Tocqueville understood that a nation with broad freedoms and small government requires a citizenry that exercises voluntary self-discipline, and that such a quality almost always derives from faith in a transcendent power. People of faith should be welcomed in the public square, not greeted with fear. Even the political opponents of religious conservatives should wish them well, because allowing them a role in government will bring us all closer to the America that Tocqueville witnessed, a nation that is strong and proud and a citizenry that is resilient and self-reliant.

Responses

1. E. J. Dionne, Jr.

I agree with some of Ralph Reed's complaints about the treatment of his movement, but in other areas I think the criticisms of the Christian Right are quite justified. To start with the area of agreement: It is entirely true that to rule religious voices out of the political debate by fiat is wrong. If America had done that in the past, the country would have been deprived of some of its most vital movements, especially movements for reform—abolitionism, the civil-rights movement, a variety of anti-war movements, much pressure for social justice and help for the poor.

Stephen Carter makes some convincing arguments on this subject in *The Culture of Disbelief.*[1] The Religious Right does need to be understood as a reaction to previous efforts to exclude traditionally religious people from public debate. The Religious Right is engaged in what Nathan Glazer has called a "defensive offensive." As Terry Eastland wrote a few years ago, "The religious person is entitled, if not to prevail, at least to be heard. The religious person can expect to be allowed a voice in matters of public policy. He can expect that his religion will not disqualify him from speaking on political matters, and that if he offers a religious or ethical justification for his position

---

E. J. Dionne, Jr., formerly a political reporter for the *New York Times,* is an editorial writer and columnist for the *Washington Post.* He is the author of *Why Americans Hate Politics.*

16

on a public issue, it will not *ipso facto* be considered out of the bounds of public discourse."[2]

Ralph Reed and his organization have a right to a place at the table, just as the Catholic bishops and the American Jewish Committee and the Southern Christian Leadership Conference and Jesse Jackson and lots of other people have that right. We need to be more honest about our reasons for ruling people in or out of the debate; it should not be done by ideological fiat. We tend to regard those religious voices we agree with as noble, moral prophets and those we disagree with as violators of the separation of church and state.

Having said this, I nonetheless think that some of the criticism of religious conservatives—to use Reed's preferred term—is justified. Reed says he's for a balanced-budget amendment, for requiring a supermajority vote in both houses of Congress to raise taxes, and for the Penny-Kasich amendment to cut federal spending. The Christian Coalition includes the support of these three proposals as part of its program. Now, I happen to be against all these things, and I also think of myself as a Christian. Respectfully I would say to Ralph Reed that I think we need to be careful about appropriating the name "Christian." It's not just a matter of "niche marketing." I think you are implying a lot if you claim to speak for Christianity and for Christians. What troubles many people is that certain planks of conservative ideology are made to seem synonymous with being Christian or being religious.

There are issues of all sorts on which Christians, like non-Christians, disagree. The balanced-budget amendment and Penny-Kasich are not matters of theology or faith. When we speak in religious terms, we need to exercise a caution that is not asked of us when we speak in purely secular terms. As far as I know, the Southern Christian Leadership Conference does not put out "Christian scorecards."

I think there is, moreover, a real fear about religious tests imposed by the majority, which in this country is a Protestant majority. While Reed himself speaks very carefully on this point, I think that some people who might be classified as "religious conservatives" or "the Religious Right" actually do believe in those tests. For example, one religious conservative who was given a prominent role in the 1984 Republican Convention was the same man who railed against John F. Kennedy in 1960, saying that his election would "spell the death of a free church in a free state," and who called the Catholic Church a political tyranny. Now 1960 is not all that long ago. People who worry about the dangers of sectarian religious pronouncements in politics are not fools or bigots. There are reasons for these worries.

I'm glad that Reed, in his paper, condemns the anti-Catholicism associated with some of the campaigns against John F. Kennedy. There has been a large and welcome change for the better in relationships between politically active Protestant conservatives on the one hand and Catholics and Jews on the other. It was very significant that in 1980, two of the candidates whom the Moral Majority worked hardest to elect were Jeremiah Denton and Don Nickles, both Roman Catholics.

In his paper, Reed criticizes the minister who said, "God does not hear the prayers of Jews," and the pamphlet that said, "To vote for Bill Clinton is a sin against God." But I think he is a little too circumspect in his criticism, and I'd like to quote what he says: these positions presented "a harsh side of religious belief that is simply inappropriate in a political context." I think religious conservatives should go further than that if they are to sustain their claim that they are not trying to impose religious tests in politics. Those positions are not just harsh—they're wrong, they're intolerant, they're mean, and they're also inconsistent with the democratic and republican spirit of our country. Similar statements have been made about gays and lesbians and feminists, to name a few groups that have been put under harsh assault by some who at least claim to speak for religious conservatism. I think that people who use the term "Christian" to describe their political beliefs really do have an obligation to behave charitably. As John Kennedy said, "Civility is not a sign of weakness."

There are indeed two sides to the culture wars, as James Davison Hunter has argued.[3] If some of the attacks *by* the Religious Right cross the line of civility, so do some of the attacks *on* the Religious Right. The fierce fights we are having on some of these issues are inevitable. The primary example is, of course, abortion. One side believes that women have a fundamental right to abortion, and the other side believes that the fetus is a human being with a fundamental right to life. It is unfair to ask either side to back down from fundamental points of principle. But I fear that we are politicizing too many moral questions. These questions need to be fought out publicly, yes, but not necessarily through the state.

Where the state is directly involved in shaping family life, whether through tax policies or through welfare policies, there is much to be brought to the political arena legitimately. One hopeful sign is that liberals and conservatives, Democrats and Republicans are coming to agree that both the tax code and the welfare system need to be more concerned about helping to keep families together and not breaking them up. But there are limits to state action, and while Reed says he believes in such limits, I'm not sure that he and his movement have always been quite so clear on that point. Specifically, there are limits to how much in the way of religious values can be brought into the public schools. The risks are not just to non-believers or to believers in minority religions, but to religious faith itself. If we do not want the public schools to embody the views of particular religious sects, neither do we want them preaching watered-down, lowest-common-denominator "faith." That ends up insulting everybody's religious convictions.

To say that the public square should be more hospitable to religious people is quite different from believing that the government itself needs to get enmeshed in religious squabbles. That is as bad for religion as it is bad for religious freedom. Civil society exists as a forum independent of government. It is the place where most of these arguments should take place. Glenn Tinder, a political philosopher who makes a lot of sense on these very difficult questions, argued in an essay written for the Ethics and Public Policy Center that the good society is a place he called "the attentive society," a place in which people "listen seriously to those with whom they fundamentally disagree." It's a place that would "provide room for strong convictions, but its defining characteristic would be a widespread willingness to give and receive assistance on the road to truth."[4] The attentive society is the only proper setting for democracy.

The purpose of democratic politics is not to provide chances to pronounce anathemas or to cast fellow citizens into darkness. To accept life in a democracy is to accept the fact that God has given none of us a monopoly on truth. As Reinhold Niebuhr said, "Man's capacity for justice makes democracy possible. Man's capacity for injustice makes democracy necessary." Especially those who use the name "Christian" to describe their politics need to remember that humility is a fundamental Christian virtue.

Responses

2. Michael Horowitz

Reading Ralph Reed's paper, I am struck by the potency and durability of the double standard applied against self-identified evangelical Christians seeking to participate in American public life. I am regularly invited to appear before Jewish social-action organizations that quite properly *insist* that their moral and political passions derive from Jewish teachings, indeed from their very Jewishness. While evangelical participation in our public life is said to pose clear dangers, Jews and Catholics are said to add much to American public life by reason of their participation in it *as Jews and Catholics.* Another example of the double standard: People for the American Way can call itself that without a whit of criticism—as if its agenda represented the sole means of achieving and strengthening the American ethos. At the same time, the Christian Coalition is angrily charged with being arrogant, and, more ominously, dangerous, when it engages in the same sort of member-enrolling organizational hype.

As I will point out later, there are reasons, and good ones, that explain and even justify today's double standard against would-be Christian political activists. Still, I think evangelical Christians have a right to resent the hypocrisy of an American elite that now actively

---

Michael Horowitz is a lawyer and a senior fellow at The Manhattan Institute. He served for six years in the Reagan administration at the Office of Management and Budget.

20

seeks to caricature and delegitimize them and in general to deny them a place in the American mainstream.

Let me begin with my central point: I believe that the elites' campaign to discredit evangelical Christians' participation in the American public square is opportunistic, venal, and downright wrong—that efforts to deny or intimidate such participation are profoundly antidemocratic and run counter to the sweep and spirit of American history. Further, I believe that evangelicals' actual participation in our public life—not merely their right to do so—represents an essential chapter in America's continuing saga of democratization. Finally, my view of the here and now of America's politics leads me to welcome the participation of evangelicals in our political life as a means of helping to restore once-vibrant common sense and moral perspectives to our public-policy debates. (I'd like to think I'd welcome evangelical participation even if I didn't feel this way, and hope I'd have as much integrity as Stephen Carter has shown in seeking to legitimate the political activism of a community with whose general views he broadly disagrees.)

My views on the need to ensure evangelical activism in American public life—both as a right (in the interest of process) and as a reality (in the interest of better public policy)—are well expressed by two writers, writing in entirely different contexts.

First, I commend to you Arthur Schlesinger's *The Age of Jackson,* a glorious treatment of a turning point in American history. Witnessing the fear and loathing now directed at evangelicals who seek to reverse their historic passivity towards politics, I am reminded of nothing so much as Schlesinger's description of the horror felt by nineteenth-century New England elites as they watched Western frontiersmen participate in Andrew Jackson's inauguration. Seeing farmers and settlers in Washington, not as awed spectators but as men and women exuberantly (actually over-exuberantly) celebrating at a White House now felt to be operating in their interests and led by one of them, the Whig elites could only describe the phenomenon as—gasp—the triumph of "KING MOB" (they even spelled it with capital letters). I'm close enough to my immigrant grandparents, to their first-generation American lives and to their formative influences on me, to feel the sting of being thought of as part of a Lower East Side tenement-dwelling MOB. It's for that reason that I take deep pride in having been part of a MOB of our times; so should evangelical Christians, for we

MOB members almost always become—after a few fits and starts and with a few rough edges rounded—the real People for the American Way.

The next publication, which didn't win *The Age of Jackson*'s Pulitzer Prize but which deserves equally wide dissemination, is Joshua Haberman's powerful *Policy Review* article, "The Bible Belt Is America's Safety Belt."[1] Haberman, a distinguished American rabbi and a survivor of Hitler's Germany, turned on its head the caricature of religious Middle Americans, who are now, shamefully, routinely portrayed as close-minded and inherently bigoted. What Haberman wrote about is what most casual travelers through the American South, Midwest, and Far West can readily find, and have from Tocqueville's time on: an open, decent people who are responsive to underdog appeals and moral claims, and instinctively hostile to unearned privilege. What Haberman wrote is what history also tells us, that family-oriented, community-minded, and religiously motivated Americans have fought the wars and paid the taxes and supported the laws and in general have been the source and secret of America's role as the "last, best hope of mankind." (The phrase is said to be that of Lincoln, our ultimate commoner.)

Of course, Haberman's people and communities are not perfectly captured by him, or by film director Frank Capra's idealized versions of decent "little guys" confounding wrongdoing and wrongdoers while still maintaining their integrity. But Capra's Gary Cooper and Jimmy Stewart characters are a darned sight closer to the truth of who we are as a nation than are such examples as the invariably bigoted leaders of religious and small-town communities who are the routine fare of today's network series and standard movies. (Ben Stein and Richard Grenier have best told the sad story of Hollywood's transmutation of what used to be our best exemplars into corrupt bad guys.[2]) Haberman saw the corruptibility of elites caught up in their own rhetoric and ambitions, saw the sturdy but quiet virtues of America's salt-of-the-earth citizens and communities, and rightly understood that our heartland and our religious faith are today's best guarantors of a civil and decent America.

Two brief and related personal tales: First, one of the most stunning "discoveries" I made when I first came into the Reagan administration was the large number of low-key, politically conservative young people who were also—shockingly—Rhodes Scholars, law-review editors,

Supreme Court law clerks, and members of similarly elite clubs and networks. But what was *really* amazing—nearly unbelievable to a consumer of establishment media like me—was the high proportion of such young people who were also committed Christians. Having been politically and morally formed when student apathy seemed the central problem of campus life (and indeed often was), and when a protesting activism was the only proper antidote, I was unprepared for moral virtue and political courage in the shape of reflective, caring young people who had been formed against the noisy, self-centered anarchies that were *their* campuses.

Moving to the present: I recently helped to host a Washington luncheon for Bret Schundler, the remarkable Jersey City mayor. Schundler is a man who, although rich, Republican, young, and white, had just swept the elections of a poor, largely minority city—and had done so on the seemingly suburban platform of lower taxes, more police, deregulation, and reduced city payrolls. Early in his luncheon talk he spoke of poor people's need for an earned dignity that only work and attachment to family and community could bring, and this was all it took for me to know that the source of his views was a deep religious commitment—in his case, as a Christian. My guess is that voters sensed that commitment and saw no proselytization in the message. My certainty is that the religiously rooted views of leaders like Schundler offer ways out of the traps now set for poor Americans by the ensnaring, perverse programs that the political system now, tragically, almost always offers.

Some Ineffectual Responses

What can be done to reduce the hostility to more active political participation by committed Christians?

First, and obviously, whining isn't the answer. Complaining about double standards and lamenting the system's bias won't do the trick. For, as George Weigel points out in his paper, politics ain't beanbag. There are still a lot of utopians of the left who want the status quo maintained in the form of a redistributionist state and a culture of radical, anti-communitarian individualism. They work very hard, they are very articulate, and they are dominant members (at times by default) of the universe of people—brilliantly described by Michael Novak as the "moral-cultural sector"[3]—who shape American ideas and values. These tough moralists know the threat posed to their politics by the entry of "conservative" religionists into American political life, and they can be expected to continue to delegitimize and caricature the views of Christian activists. But grumbling about this won't accomplish much.

Nor will the John Kennedy analogy be useful, except to persuade evangelicals to complain even more about their lot. Kennedy's famous speech to Texas preachers, to which Ralph Reed refers, was that of a man who reassured us not to worry about his Catholicism *because it would have no impact on his politics or public-policy views.* Don't worry about my Catholicism, Kennedy pretty nearly said, because it stops at the church door, because the Pope's teaching on ritual, on which ring to kiss on what finger, represents the sole area of his authority or influence over me. Kennedy's speech would be relevant to Ralph Reed's situation if Reed were to say that his members, organized because they were Christians, held the full spectrum of views on whether to lock up violent criminals for long or short prison terms, on whether abortion was good or bad, on whether or not to legalize drugs, on what sort of social-science approaches made the most sense for America's students. If the Kennedy analogy were apt, all that Reed would need to ask was that the American public not discriminate against some of his members because they practiced foot-washing in their churches. Ralph Reed's organization, and other Christian political activists, of course seek more than passive non-discrimination against churchgoers; theirs is a pro-active agenda that seeks to incorporate moral and political values derived from Christian convictions into our decision-making processes. Therefore it won't do for Ralph Reed to complain about being treated differently than JFK was.

Let's try again. What promise is offered by what can fairly be called the "rhetorical approach"? Some, I think, but much less, I fear, than what many seem to believe.

Of course it is terribly important not to alienate others unduly through the use of words and phrases that convey more (or less) than one means. Of course everyone can profit from techniques and strategies that help us better communicate what we want to say, that generate "warm," not frightening, auras to the intended audiences.

I remember talking with James Watt, the lightning-rod Secretary of the Interior under Reagan, a man I knew to be deeply affected, indeed scarred, by the Holocaust. (I had seen this in a variety of private, non-political moments.) With considerable pride, Watt had sent me an advance copy of a speech he was to give to the annual assembly of his evangelical church. The speech began with moving references to the Holocaust and the need to remember its victims and causes and to ensure that it never happened again. I was much taken with what I was reading, and couldn't wait to show it to friends whose de-monized view of Watt, I thought, would be much shaken by his manifest conviction on a subject they never dreamed he cared about.

So I thought, that is, until I came to the lines that directly followed the speech's discussion of the Nazi era. "But the Holocaust still continues," read the segue line. "I refer, of course, to the abortions now routinely taking place in America." I called Watt and urged him at least to separate his discussions of Hitler and *Roe* v. *Wade* by a few pages or so. I told him that he was about to lose non-church audiences he might otherwise reach, and that he could avoid doing this without moderating his views on abortion. I told him that there were deeply caring people (my wife, for example) who grieved over people lost in concentration camps *and* supported the right to abortion, and that they would never accept the genuineness of his views about the former if he acted as if it were no different from the latter. Just separate the two segments of your speech, I pleaded, out of sensitivity to people who disagree with you on the abortion question. I failed, because what to Jim Watt were the horrors of abortion were no less vividly felt by him than the horrors of the Holocaust. In making the speech, Watt thus forfeited the chance to persuade people outside his church that he cared about much beside abortion, and wound up, ironically, confirming for many the false view of him as insensitive if not anti-Semitic.

There are other buzzword traps to avoid in Christian communica-tion with non-believing and non-Christian audiences, and avoiding them can do much good. Michael Farris gives some of these in his response to George Weigel's paper [chapter 3]. But the larger point I wish to make is that mere rhetorical techniques will not significantly abate the antipathy and suspicion now confronted by even the best of good, caring Christians. Farris's approach, with its reliance on imag-inative ways to use language to reach and reassure hostile listeners, is useful only up to a point—a fact that I believe was sadly confirmed by the demagogic success of his electoral opponent in radically misdescribing who he was during his unsuccessful 1993 race for Virginia lieutenant governor.

What then to do? Is there anything beside bias and politically manipulated elite scheming that explains why Ralph Reed is so regularly asked the "but what do you *really* believe" question? In fact, I believe that *there are legitimate bases for concerns, rooted in sad, inescapable historical truths, about would-be political actors who are both conservative and Christian.* These historical truths are, in my view, ignored only at the peril of groups like the Christian Coalition that seek mainstream political status. As they struggle for a place on the moral high ground that (happily for America) all groups must occupy if they are to be taken seriously in our politics, those who are both conservative and Christian need to realize that critical historical facts subject them to a powerful double whammy.

The Conservative Handicap

Let's take the conservative handicap first, and let's examine it by using a key segment of Ralph Reed's paper. Reed writes of what he takes to be the modest and unexceptionable basic desire of religious conservatives to return to an America many of us grew up in—a post–World War II country that was proud of itself, was militarily strong, and had a clear moral compass. The breakpoint in this once-American reality, Reed notes, not incorrectly, was the mid-sixties. His lament is thus a reasonable one. *And yet!* The mid-sixties were precisely the time when we embarked on our great, critical, necessary-for-our-very-decency-as-a-nation struggle to end racial injustice in America. And this was a struggle in which conservatives as a whole were at best indifferent and for the most part were on the wrong side. One reason why you'll find no liberals more committed than Southern liberals is that, as they lived through the civil-rights revolution, the label "conservative" was a common descriptor of people who wanted to maintain separate drinking fountains, to keep segregation alive, to defend racism. Whatever the depredations that liberals may have committed over the past twenty-five years against the interests of poor people and racial minorities—and they have been many and are profound—liberals were at least on the right side, on the side of the Constitution, on the just and moral side, when the critical pre- and post–*Brown* v. *Board of Education* battles were fought.

Overcoming such a real burden of history will take much frank acknowledgment, however decent we may now believe ourselves as conservatives to be (and however decent we may in fact be). It may require us to acknowledge—and not in the form of debaters' devices, either—that it was good for the American left to have succeeded, and good for the American right to have lost, in the historic struggles that gave black Americans the right to vote and freed them from state-imposed racism.

In my view, our past compels us not merely to tolerate but to *insist on* the liberals' preferred frame of reference for public-policy debates: that policies should be judged by the measure of hope and opportunity they offer the poorest and most needful Americans, by the extent to which they successfully complete Abraham Lincoln's revolution, and not by how much more comfortable they make those of us who are already so. (This is a standard that should not be hard for Christians to adopt!) Given the record of the past twenty-five years or so, these are also debates we are sure to win. It should not be hard to make clear, as Myron Magnet[4] and Michael Novak,[5] among others, have done: (1) that free markets offer the best if not the only real means of escape from poverty and from feudal entrapment in the status of our parents; and (2) that anything-goes, radical individualism, whatever mixed blessings it may bring to middle-class and wealthy Americans, creates and destroys poor and underclass Americans who lack private resources, families, and value systems to fall back on.

That an American left, which professes to speak for the poor, has supported values and policies that have decimated their would-be beneficiaries thus opens the door for a debate that should establish the clear *bona fides* of conservatives and conservative policies. But this is not a debate we can win merely by being right. We conservatives must first show that we understand how we are seen by others and, given much of our history, why this is so.

The Christian Handicap

If the conservative handicap is great, however, the Christian one is greater—by orders of magnitude.

I say this as one who has watched Christians explode with anger, shake their heads in puzzlement, or think that nothing is in play save double standards and vicious politics when their public professions of

Christian belief lead to veiled (and often unveiled) charges of anti-Semitism. Why is it, I have heard conservative politicians from presidents on down ask, that my attendance at a prayer breakfast leads to public rumblings that concentration camps are on the way? After all, people with active, living Christian faiths know who they are and what they feel, know the profound untruth, the preposterousness of such charges. They also see so-called Third World leaders (and others in America, such as Jesse Jackson) escape relatively unscathed after engaging in openly anti-Semitic conduct that would have forever destroyed *their* political careers. And they know how little credit they receive for their deep commitment on such issues as Israel's strength and well-being, and for the active outreach efforts of many into ghetto slums that few politically correct social-service organizations would even think of entering. They think that all this should make a difference, wonder why it so often doesn't, and finally give up trying to figure it all out except to think of themselves as slandered victims.

How, then, *can* charges that are so untrue ring so loudly and with such sheer political force? Here again I believe the critical answers are to be found through an examination of history. It is a history of Christian norms and conduct that, if unknown, misunderstood, or unacknowledged by evangelical leaders, will entrap them into permanent demonization by the media and their political adversaries.

At the heart of the legitimacy problem suffered by Christians seeking to engage in the political process is their failure to understand the frightening conduct of past generations of committed Christians. Most American Jews are second- or third-generation Americans, and many have heard direct accounts from parents and grandparents of what it was like to hide in cellars from Easter Sunday pogroms, or barely to escape similar acts of terrorism that were religiously led or based. There are, moreover, fair numbers of American stories of religious and religiously inspired intolerance—from the Salem witch trials to the Scopes trial, from the Leo Frank case to personal accounts such as mine of being beaten up on the way home from school with the charge that "you killed our Christ." German evangelicals gave critical early support to Hitler—and did so, by the way, on the very restore-morality-to-government-and-society grounds that are the stated basis of the Christian Coalition's involvement in politics. The Dietrich Bonhoeffers were in a distinct minority, overwhelmed by those who aided Hitler in the very name of Christian renewal.

This, then, is the seamier historical side of Christian belief and of Christian action come to political power, and it is this history that more than anything else arms those who would keep conservative Christians forever illegitimate and out of power.

But what of the fact that past patterns no longer hold, that organized churches are today powerful bastions against such conduct and are no longer, save in fugitive, anecdotal cases, means of support for hatred and bigotry? Today's Christians are right to say that this is so, and Joshua Haberman is right in making his Bible Belt–Safety Belt connection, *but this is precisely why Christians must now deal with their past.* Doing so would allow present-day Christian leaders to make the point that lessons have been learned, that Christianity has changed. It would allow Ralph Reed and his colleagues to say credibly to the American political community at large what I know to be true: that the committed Christian in a post-Holocaust world would be the one who is first to sew the yellow star on his sleeve. Such acknowledgment would take much of the sting out of elite attacks on the moral standing of evangelicals and would help open-minded Americans realize that evangelical participation in mainstream American political life will not involve threatening specters and hidden agendas. It would do even more by allowing dissemination of a powerful truth that also needs to be known: that in today's world, anti-Semitism and most other comparable ideologies of bigotry are, in almost complete reversal of the pre-Holocaust fact of life, a phenomenon of the political left, not the "conservative" political right.

Three Liberating Steps

I believe there are three critical steps for Christian conservatives to take to demonstrate their liberation from the dybbuks of their past.

Step one: they need to lighten up a bit, to understand that while some of the barbs directed at them are venal, it is also in the nature of things for rookies breaking into the big leagues to be hazed and unfairly tested. Say what you will about the elites who dominate and run our media and politics, about their arrogance, the terrible mistakes they have made, the unjust and self-serving and hypocritical burdens they have imposed—I've at times said all that, and then some—but it's also fair to say that it's still a darned good country that they run. They won't easily turn this country over to an untested MOB, and they will exploit every possible element of conservative Christians' past, will try to get them to rise to the bait in ways that will show they are too easily rattled to take a major hand in running the country.

It's hard to tell people not to take it personally when their integrity is routinely assaulted and their record routinely distorted, and I surely don't mean to counsel a course of passive surrender for Christians in the public square. Rather, my suggestion is that they go about their business more coolly, less angrily, and with a confidence born of the fact that 25 per cent of the American electorate must in the fullness of time have its place in the political sun, its chance to convert social needs into political realities. But the sooner conservative Christians play politics as Jackie Robinson first played with the Brooklyn Dodgers —regularly swallowing what later turned out to be a world-class pride, working harder than anyone else, competing with greater energy *and fairness* than his adversaries, getting even rather than getting mad—the sooner the general American public will reject their critics and actively welcome their efforts to shape and change the political process.

Step two: I suggest that evangelicals seek a particularly intense dialogue with the American Jewish community—if only to help ensure that they can no longer be easily used as bloody-shirt symbols with which increasing numbers of Jewish waverers from liberal orthodoxy can be frightened into a return to the fold. Moreover, as Jews have been the key historic targets of Christian bigotry (or, as some would put it, litmus indicators of the extent to which Christian beliefs are truly held by professing Christians), increased comfort levels between evangelicals and Jews would reassure others from outside the Jewish community about evangelicals. One caveat: Beware of philo-Semitism as a means of reassuring Jews of Christian good will. For Christians to say they seek fellowship with Jews because the Bible teaches them to do so is at best unpersuasive; being told by an evangelical that one is loved because one is a Jew is for most of us as spooky as being the object of good old-fashioned anti-Semitism. It's more than enough for modern-day Christians to persuade Jews that lessons have been learned from the past, that Christian beliefs will never again be a route to hate; singling Jews out as special objects of Christian attention sends out troublesome signals to Jews, no matter how favorable the attention is meant to be.

Finally, and critically, step three: I urge evangelicals to resist the impulse to demonize those with whom they disagree over the moral and cultural issues that brought them into politics. Look, for example, to James Q. Wilson, exquisitely fair and balanced as always, for a formulation of the issues in play in today's politics. To Wilson, the battle is not (as some of us have occasionally put it) between philistines seeking to tear things down and those of us seeking to restore decency and basic values. Wilson instead talks of today's central issue as a contest between competing cultures of self-expression and self-discipline.[6] Precisely because we want our children to be both disciplined and expressive, Wilson's formulation forces us to see today's cultural and political wars not as wars between good and evil but as the more subtle business of choosing the side we wish most to err on. There needs to be greater acknowledgment that the other side of the debate has morally and philosophically respectable claims, and recognition of this fact should inform evangelical participation in the political process.

Such benign detachment toward political adversaries will not always occur, of course, particularly in the white heat of battle and during election campaigns and legislative and litigation struggles. Nor should it. But the core virtues of today's liberals, freedom and expressiveness, should almost always be visible, if at times from afar, as *virtues*. Such a view of their political adversaries can and should always be a perspective that Christians in politics regularly note. Doing so will help to rebut the claims that they are dangerous, are intolerant of other views, and seek to impose their will (if not their religion) whenever they achieve political power. These claims are the chief means of delegitimating Christians' political participation and the chief present barrier to their entry into the political mainstream.

The point I have tried to make is that these claims need to be both understood and diminished—a process that I am confident is now proceeding apace.

Comments

Ralph Reed: I want to underscore my agreement that we have to be very careful about linking the name of Christ with a partisan political agenda, left or right. We in the Christian Coalition don't think that someone who disagrees with our political agenda is somehow not a Christian, or that becoming a Christian requires you to accept that political agenda. I believe that principles derived from faith and Scripture can be applied to issues, but I don't believe that a specific political agenda, whether left, right, or center, can be considered the Christian agenda. When Christ came down off the mountain and selected twelve disciples, he included Matthew, who was a tax gatherer with the oppressive Roman Empire, and Simon, a member of the party that was trying to overthrow the Roman government through violent forms of terrorism. It would be a little like selecting a secessionist and an abolitionist in the 1850s, or selecting Pat Robertson and Jesse Jackson today.

I also agree with what Michael Horowitz said about anti-Semitism: the past does matter, and we need more dialogue on that.

Richard Land: That kind of dialogue needs to take place and in some places has taken place. It has been much more pervasive on civil rights, which was, of course, a far more immediate issue for evangelical churches in the South. A lot of people in those churches have ac-

---

Note: These participants are identified on pages 117-18.

knowledged that the treatment of blacks was wrong, and have done so repeatedly. It has been a real healing process.

But we, as leaders in the conservative movement, need to do a better job of helping our people understand the sense of grievance that both African-Americans and Jewish people have. In a recent symposium on race relations, one of our black pastors said, "I just don't think you realize how badly you have hurt us." We can't repent of our forebears' sins, because we're not Mormons, but we can say we're sorry for the grief that was caused. We can also take some extraordinary steps to try to bridge the gulf created by that difficult historical experience. I'm somewhat aware of continuing prejudice in this country, and I suspect that I would be far, far more aware of it if my skin were a different color or if I were Jewish.

I think it would be difficult to overestimate the importance of what we are talking about. If we are going to have a rebuilding of an American culture of value and significance, it is going to take a real coalition of Catholics, evangelical Protestants both black and white, and conservative Jews, at least, plus any others who want to come along. Whether we can do that will depend on whether we can resolve the kinds of issues that are being raised here. There is in our culture a sort of a "squishy middle" that is up for grabs. The group that is able to articulate its vision for the future in a way that captures the moral imagination of that squishy middle will prevail.

Marshall Wittman: I have a unique perspective on this dialogue, being Jewish and working for the Christian Coalition. Dennis Prager, a noted Jewish commentator, has said that the Jewish mind is paralyzed by Christian anti-Semitism, much as the black mind is paralyzed by memories of white racism. I grew up in Waco, Texas (pre-Koresh), which is a very religious, very Southern Baptist community, and there is a close relationship between the Jewish community and the Christian community there. The fears of Christian anti-Semitism today are essentially unwarranted, but I know that they are based in history. I'm reminded of it every time I talk to my mother.

About the Coalition's "Congressional Scorecard": as one who helps to put together the Scorecard and who is not of the Christian faith, I can assure everyone that its purpose is not to make a judgment about who is a good Christian and who is not. Nor do we ever suggest in our rhetoric that that is the case. The issues we include are basic ones.

Last spring, during the budget debate, we ran some radio advertisements in selected districts about the Clinton tax plan. We never suggested it was anti-Christian—we said it didn't make economic sense. A congressman from Ohio suggested that we had called him un-Christian. Nothing of the sort had ever taken place.

To suggest that it is inappropriate for us to take on issues like the tax plan amounts to a kind of self-ghettoization: we should be involved only in certain social issues and should stay out of others. We know that Jewish organizations and other religious organizations weigh in on a range of issues. My first job out of college was with the United Farm Workers; I worked for Cesar Chavez, so you can see that I've taken a long political odyssey myself. At that time we were heavily supported by the archdiocese of Detroit. We had farm-worker Masses in the churches in Detroit. My room and board were paid for by the archdiocese. But no one ever saw this as some kind of Catholic conspiracy. I never heard such a charge from a liberal columnist or from a conservative columnist. Well, twenty years later I'm working for the Christian Coalition, and hardly a day passes in which I don't hear that it is inappropriate for us to weigh in on an issue because of the name of our organization, or the faith of most of the people who are members of it.

George Weigel: I'm not terribly comforted by the political activities of other ostensibly religious organizations. Some Jewish organizations have essentially reduced themselves to ethnic interest groups with virtually no religious content. When Joseph Lowery of the Southern Christian Leadership Conference speaks, people don't hear a Christian minister: they hear a liberal, Democratic political operator. Period. The SCLC today isn't what it was during the Montgomery bus boycott. If you're concerned not simply about political effectiveness but about the integrity of the Church, the integrity of the Gospel, then be very careful about looking at those examples as ways of being the public church. What has happened, time and time again, is that an increasingly partisan public profile ends up stripping an organization of religiously based moral content.

Ralph Reed: What about when Martin Luther King, as head of the Southern Christian Leadership Conference, spoke out against the Vietnam war? He wasn't speaking out only against segregation; he was also opposing the war.

George Weigel: My point is about the trajectory of these organizations over time and the great danger of corrupting religious witness when that witness focuses so intensely on partisan questions. When you try to broaden the agenda, it isn't clear what is a first-order moral judgment, and what is a second-, third-, or fourth-order pragmatic prudential judgment that may have some slight connection to Christian moral understanding but is in no sense as morally or religiously urgent. Term limits are not as urgent as abortion. To suggest that everything from voting rights for the delegate from Guam to *Roe* v. *Wade* is part of a Christian agenda demeans the whole agenda and takes away from the urgency of the really important front-burner issues.

E. J. Dionne: Richard Land said there is a squishy middle up for grabs. I would like to make the case that the middle isn't squishy; in fact, there is a kind of reaction to politics in this country as it has been practiced for a long time, which a lot of people see as a fight of liberals and conservatives over which set of sins matters the most. People react against that very argument. I think that the middle, rather than being squishy, comprises two impulses that aren't necessarily contradictory to each other. One is a deep uneasiness about the country's moral direction, especially about violence, family breakup, and fatherless kids, and a desire to grapple with those problems. The response to President Clinton's Memphis speech in November 1993 suggests just how far across the political spectrum that concern goes. At the same time I think there is great reluctance to go back to the 1950s, to overturn the gains made by feminism and civil rights, the decrease in anti-Semitism and anti-Catholicism. There is also a reluctance to see abortion banned entirely, or to see gays pushed back in the closet. I think that this middle believes these two sets of things rather strongly.

George Weigel: Christianity is not essentially a instrument for doing this world's business. When it has made itself that, it has gotten into trouble time and time again. The question is, How do we have this vibrant, religiously informed, morally urgent, sharp-edged type of witness without falling into the trap of simply making Christian conviction another instrumental force in a world of instrumentality?

Michael Farris: I applaud Michael Horowitz's statements about the need for evangelical Christians to show that they understand. Part of the reason why that isn't done much is that we don't study history all that much. I grew up as a Baptist in Washington state. I knew nothing of the daily struggle of racial discrimination; and we were taught to honor the Jewish tradition so much that I almost felt cheated for not being Jewish. Somehow that understanding has to go both ways. I know that the victimization that blacks and Jews experienced was far more grievous than anything that evangelical Christians are experiencing today. Nonetheless, evangelicals do feel victimized by today's culture, the political culture and the media in particular. I predict that twenty years from now evangelicals will be saying to the editors and editorial boards of this country: We want you to understand how deeply we were offended by that period when you treated us with religious bigotry.

One of the most rewarding things I have ever done was to work at the very center of the Religious Freedom Restoration Act with Marc Stern, general counsel of the American Jewish Congress. He and I were co-chairmen of the drafting committee. Eventually every major Jewish organization and every major religious organization from right to left lined up on that bill. We showed that we could work together and make some good things happen for this country. We do have some common traditions, and we do have some things we won't put up with. I took a lot of flak from conservatives for consorting with the ACLU and with other liberal organizations. But if a group stays with the common American tradition of freedom and lack of bias and lack of bigotry, we ought to fight together for those things.

Clarke Cochran: I don't object to the Religious Right's taking a position on a wide range of issues. But I do object to taking the secular conservative agenda and stamping it "Christian" without any theological or philosophical analysis. Why should a Christian accept these particular positions? A lot of issues that Christians should be supporting, such things as gun control, justice in health care, protecting the vulnerable widows and orphans (to use biblical language), dignified work for people, and property for the common good (from the Catholic natural-law tradition), never appear because the religious groups, in this case the Christian Coalition, have been captured by the conservative ideological position. Their positions simply reflect that, rather than engaging in a religious, philosophical, theological analysis of the issues and arriving at independent judgments. The problem is the package. If on a range of issues some of the positions were conservative and some liberal, one would guess that those positions were based on some analysis beyond simply accepting the whole ideological package.

Clyde Wilcox: Ralph Reed's new position on abortion—abolish *Roe* and leave it to the states—would allow states to codify *Roe*. Indeed, some states have already done so, and California has found *Roe* guarantees in the state constitution. So really, Reed's new position is just a states' rights position, which is what George McGovern supported in 1972.

Ralph Reed: I do not accept that interpretation of what I said. I think I called *Roe* v. *Wade* the most unwise act of judicial fiat since *Dred Scott*. I did not say that I would favor any state's codifying *Roe* v. *Wade*. What I said was that I was against taking the laws of the only two states that had abortion-on-demand at the time of the decision and imposing those laws on all the other states.

James Guth: Will the real Christian Coalition please stand up? Is its true nature more like that of its executive director, Ralph Reed, or the activist I heard at the Coalition's national convention responding to both the Democratic National Chairman and other speakers in ways that I thought did not reflect the broadened and more moderate policy stand?

Michael Bauman: When I speak in the public square, I cannot and I must not permit the offended sensibilities of the left to veto my language or my position, just as they don't let my offended sensibility veto theirs. I have to have access to all my words and all my arguments. I have to protect my freedom of speech. I have to be able to call things by their real names. If I talked the same way about all issues, I'd be treating things that are evil the same way I treat things that are good. That's why sometimes I feel I must reject the softer rhetoric, because it feels so much like dissembling. And that may help to explain why James Guth and others sometimes have a hard time figuring out the Religious Right.

Terry Eastland: I would like to throw into the mix a slightly different idea. I suggest that there is more commonality than we might think between the Religious Right and many in the mainstream today. Let's take the issue of rights. Michael Farris mentioned how proud he was of his involvement in drafting the Religious Freedom Restoration Act. That act is a legislative response to the Supreme Court's peyote decision, as it is called—the 1990 *Smith* case out of Oregon. The coalition working to pass RFRA cut across the religious spectrum and included people of the Religious Right as well as those who might be called the Religious Left. It included all sorts of secular groups, too —even People for the American Way, which at the time was locked in litigation with Michael Farris in the *Mozert* case. And in fact, we know from Stephen Bates's excellent book on that subject, *Battleground,* that People for the American Way rejected the kind of legal standard that was embraced by Justice Scalia in the majority opinion in the *Smith* case.

We talk about recovering the principles of the 1950s. If we were to recover those principles, we would have a different understanding of the free-exercise clause. The standard that has just been enacted by RFRA is new to our constitutional law; it was given to us in a 1963 case, twenty-seven years before it was taken away in the *Smith* case. I'm trying to suggest that there is a commonality of vocabulary and interests. The language of rights, the language of equality—this is the vocabulary I hear being used by persons like Michael Farris on the Religious Right, and it seems to me to point to a different future rather than pointing back to the fifties. I see the possibility of creating new structures that we haven't seen before in our politics. Think of George Gilder's idea of microcosm. Think of using school-choice systems to start new schools, not building schools on the ruins of the public educational system.

Michael Horowitz: The real argument against the elite political culture of ever-expanding rights is simply that it hasn't worked. It has had perverse effects, and its most perverse effects have been on its intended beneficiaries. In the courts, due-process hearing rights before public-school discipline can be administered, before public-housing evictions can be made, before the mentally ill can be taken off the streets—these combined with the striking down of the so-called vagrancy laws, which has had the effect of radically reducing the ability of street cops to tell disruptive people to move on and to break up street-corner drug bazaars and crack houses—have had devastating effects on community stability and the development of community leadership in our urban ghetto.

As for the political system's so-called War on Poverty: I worked at the Office of Management and Budget for over six years, and I saw all too clearly the gap between the rhetoric and the reality of who really benefits from those programs. Every time I saw kids marching outside protesting Reagan administration policies on the grounds that the rich and the powerful had too much power, I wanted to go out and join them and lead the parade, because they didn't know the half of it. They didn't know the extent to which these counterproductive programs were enriching the rich and the powerful. Instead of giving money to the poor, we gave money to service providers in the hope that it would trickle down and benefit the poor, which it did not.

E. J. Dionne: I also think that our politics is becoming more liberal at a time when our culture is becoming more conservative. President Clinton, certainly in what he says, reflects that. And some of the people in his administration, like Bruce Reed and William Galston, speak a virtue language about social policy and also about the limits of social policy.

Michael Barone: The Charles Murray article in the *Wall Street Journal* ["The Coming White Underclass," Oct. 29, 1993] reinforces Michael Horowitz's point that the rights-based welfare state has not worked. And not only has it failed to work, but it has helped to produce this horrifying criminal underclass, where armed males go about and kill other males and use sexually any females they want. This is a condition of life in every large American city; the results of it are on view on every television newscast. It presents us with an opportunity, politically, but also with a huge responsibility to come up with something better.

One thing that needs to be done is to replace the culture of the caregivers, the products of the graduate schools of social work and education, which are the incubators of bad ideas. These are people we are paying taxes to support, the people being paid $75,000 to $100,000 to produce these horrifying neighborhoods. They should have no moral capital left at this time. How do we shift the responsibility for supplying social services to people who will teach better moral lessons than the current caregivers, who are constantly playing out their own adolescent rebellion against middle-class values?

Stephen Monsma: I'm continually frustrated by the idea that we have to choose between a big bureaucratic welfare state and doing nothing. I see a third way in something that Jack Kemp and others have been talking about: the use of non-profit organizations, many of which would be religiously based, to empower people. It's the old Neuhaus/Berger idea of mediating structures [*To Empower People: The Role of Mediating Structures in Public Policy,* by Peter L. Berger and Richard John Neuhaus, 1977]. There are ideas like that out there, and I hope that the Christian Coalition does more than what it has done to pursue these ideas and really develop a third way.

Michael Horowitz: I agree completely that the third way, helping people through voluntary organizations, is a highly important means of social-service delivery. The whole history of the Great Society was that money, rather than going directly to the poor, went to organizations that used to be voluntary but had been profoundly captured by government. Only one major institution wasn't captured by government, didn't become an arm of government, and that was the Catholic Church, which, through no lack of trying on its part, couldn't get any money from the government. The wall-of-separation constructs of the courts ironically permitted Catholic church schools to survive and flourish and to educate ghetto kids for a few thousand dollars a year when the public schools were failing at a $10,000-per-year cost.

On reflection, as I look at the whole experience of the Catholic Church's not being dependent on hustling for government grants, I would be as tough on First Amendment funding issues, as tough in preserving walls of separation, as any of the liberals have ever been, but for the opposite reason. The First Amendment is there not so much to protect us from religion as to protect religion from us. To those who are enamored of school voucher programs I say: be very, very careful.

I recall being in the Cabinet room during a discussion of what the government should do to please the Right to Life people. The Secretary of Health and Human Services said something like this: "I know what we can do. All hospitals are getting Medicare and Medicaid, so we'll just regulate the hospitals. We'll limit the right to perform abortions of any hospital that takes a patient under Medicare or Medicaid." I tried to say, "This is not direct money to the hospitals; these are people with a voucher for health care. Why are you corrupting private institutions?" But that argument sounded pretty silly and abstract to most people when the Right to Life groups were breathing heavily down the necks of the Reagan administration and we had to produce some results. My advice is, if you want to create private institutions that aren't in partnership with but rather are competitors of government, be very, very wary of voucher programs or any other programs where government funds are given.

Richard Land: I agree completely. I have told Baptist churches everywhere that if vouchers pass, don't take them, because unless you are the National Endowment for the Arts, with government money come government strings. The NEA seems to be the one exception to that. We'll end up getting government regulation and will have sold our soul for a pittance.

I don't think any of us want to go back to the 1950s or even the 1960s. My children watch a lot of old television series, because they are the only ones we let them watch, and I am embarrassed and somewhat pained by the childlike and dependent nature that women are portrayed as having in these series. They are almost as foolish as men are in current sitcoms. I don't think any of us want to go back to Ozzie and Harriet, and certainly we don't want to go back to the days when there was such intense insensitivity on racism. Something else will have to emerge. Edward R. Norman has said that pluralism is the name a society gives itself when it's in the process of transition from one orthodoxy to another. I think we will be making some very basic decisions by the end of this decade. A lot of people didn't want civil rights, and they were willing to kill to keep civil-rights bills from passing. But we didn't wait for an overwhelming consensus to do what we thought was right. I still hold out the civil-rights movement as evidence that this culture can come to some decisions about what's right and what's wrong and act accordingly. The Civil Rights Act didn't reflect the majority opinion in Mississippi or Alabama or Georgia or North Carolina or Texas, but by God we did it.

Ralph Reed: I want to make it perfectly clear that I do not want to go back to the 1950s. In my paper I said that "religious conservatives want to move forward, not backward. We believe that some of the social changes of the past thirty years are advances that must be preserved." I specifically mentioned advances for minorities and women. What we want to do is recapture a vision of America that encompasses much of what was good about America for the first hundred years of the republic—not to recapture the bad but to bring some of the good back to where we are today.

Michael Horowitz: I think there is something inherently religious in much of what the Christian Coalition is trying to do. They are calling for individual accountability and for a lesser state, and they are seeking to be agents of change. That's what religious people ought to be, challengers of the status quo. I am impressed at Ralph Reed's success in dealing with the heavy bias against his organization's very right to be, and in organizing an extraordinary, potentially very powerful coalition.

E. J. Dionne: As Jack Kemp likes to say, we are a liberal, democratic society, small *l,* small *d.* Americans identify with the small *l* and the small *d* words. A liberal, democratic society presents a certain challenge to religious people, because religious people believe, fundamentally, that they have truth with a capital *T.* But the liberal, democratic society asserts that its functioning depends upon a contest of ideas. It refuses to establish in its own practices and in its government certain things that religious people take for granted. This is a continuing source of friction.

2

Murphy Brown Revisited:
The Social Issues in the
1992 Election

John C. Green, James L. Guth,
Lyman A. Kellstedt, and Corwin E. Smidt

Early interpretations of the 1992 presidential election contain a myth: that religious conservatives cost George Bush many votes, if not the election, by saddling him with unpopular social issues, from abortion to "family values."[1] The prominence of Pat Buchanan and Pat Robertson at the Republican National Convention became the touchstone of this myth.[2] Even analysts who thought that poor economic conditions explained the election outcome saw social issues and their advocates as detrimental to the Republicans.[3] All such assessments share the assumption that, as one analyst put it, religious conservatives are an "extremist (and extremely small)" bloc of single-minded social-issue voters, out of step with the rest of the country.[4]

While not without some factual basis, these views reveal a misun-

John C. Green is associate professor of political science at the University of Akron and director of the Ray C. Bliss Institute of Applied Politics. **James L. Guth** is professor of political science at Furman University. **Lyman A. Kellstedt** is professor of political science at Wheaton College (Illinois). **Corwin E. Smidt** is professor of political science at Calvin College.

derstanding of the role of religion in politics and, more generally, of the nature of electoral coalitions. The 1992 National Election Study (NES) carried out by the University of Michigan offers some solid information relevant to these questions.[5] Its data suggest to us that: (1) religious voting blocs were very important in 1992, despite the enormous impact of economic distress; (2) George Bush gained more votes than he lost on social issues, but these gains were dwarfed by his losses from the economy; and (3) Christian Right activists may have helped mobilize their constituency for the Republican ticket.

ELECTORAL COALITIONS AND RELIGION

American elections are commonly said to be characterized by coalitions, but the implications of this truism are often ignored. Simply put, an electoral coalition is a set of voting blocs joined in support of a candidate or party.[6] Voting blocs consist of citizens with common characteristics and interests who can be mobilized on the basis of these commonalities. Although voter mobilization is a complex subject, a central feature is the use of issues to link voting blocs to candidates and parties. This linkage has two facets: voters' positions on the issues, and the priority they assign to these issues.[7] The *positions* provide a basis for the vote, while the *priority* motivates voting on that basis.

Of course, the notoriously low levels of attention, information, and opinion consistency in the American public reduce the *direct* impact of issues on voting; much of their influence occurs indirectly through partisanship, group attachments, symbolic appeals, and candidate images.[8] Hence any measure of the direct impact of issues on voting probably understates their importance to coalition-building.

We can thus identify three elements of electoral coalitions useful for our purposes: voting blocs, issue positions linking blocs to candidates and parties, and issue priorities activating these links. If all voting blocs agreed on issue positions and priorities, or if one bloc were large enough to win on its own, a coalition would not be necessary. But in the absence of such conditions, candidates and parties must attract voters with differing issue positions and priorities. Successful coalitions turn collections of minorities into "artificial" majorities or pluralities. Thus, even small groups of voters may be crucial to a candidate's success at the polls.

The great diversity of American society, coupled with constitutional arrangements that both encourage pluralism and sharply reduce the avenues to national elected office, makes coalitions nearly inevitable. And historically, the most durable basis for such coalitions has been religious traditions—that is, sets of denominations and churches with similar beliefs, practices, and origins.[9] Since early in the nineteenth century, the culturally dominant Protestant churches have been the core of one major electoral coalition, lodged first in the Whig Party and then in the Republican Party, while their culturally subordinate rivals, including sectarian Protestants, Catholics, Jews, and non-religious persons, coalesced in the other coalition, located in the Democratic Party.[10] Although the composition and strength of these alliances have varied over time and place and according to salient issues, religious tradition has persistently been among the most powerful influences on the vote.[11]

More than two-thirds of the U.S. adult population is identified with three major religious traditions. Throughout most of the twentieth century, what we now call **Mainline Protestants** have been the culturally dominant religious tradition. Characterized by a willingness to accommodate orthodox Protestant beliefs to the modern world, this group has declined in influence and size in recent decades; it now accounts only for some 20 per cent of the adult population, and perhaps less.[12] Meanwhile, what we now call **Evangelical Protestants**, churches that resisted accommodation to the modern world and remained committed to orthodox Protestant beliefs, have grown in influence and size and now make up some 25 per cent of the adult population. The third major tradition, **Roman Catholics**, has faced many of the same stresses that have divided Protestants but has nevertheless grown in influence and size; it now accounts for 24 per cent of the adult population.

Other smaller groups have been important as well. The non-religious population has become a significant voting bloc only recently; at least 15 per cent of U.S. adults, and perhaps twice that many, can be classified as **Seculars**. A host of smaller religious traditions together account for 16 per cent of the adult population. These include black Protestants and Christian denominations outside the major traditions (such as the Eastern Orthodox Churches), plus Jews and other non-Christian groups. In the tables that follow, these groups will be designated **Other Traditions**.

The historic voting patterns among these religious traditions are still evident today, though they have been modified somewhat by the turmoil of the past three decades. The Republican coalition is centered on white Protestants: the Mainline Protestants are increasingly joined by Evangelical Protestants, who are moving away from the Democratic Party. The Democratic coalition is build around Catholics, Jews, black Protestants, and Seculars, with many of the latter having shifted away from the Protestant Mainline and the GOP.[13]

The enduring religious underpinnings of electoral coalitions strongly suggest that culture is the foundation of American politics, and that rival sets of beliefs, world views, and lifestyles set the bounds of consensus and conflict.[14] This view runs against the conventional wisdom, which posits economic conflict and class solidarity as the foundations of politics. While both cultural and economic factors clearly influence election returns, the former represent long-term influences and the latter short-term factors. Culture and religion are deeply embedded in the way people are raised and live their lives, and such influences change only gradually. Indeed, from this perspective, social class is as much a cultural phenomenon as a material one.[15] Economic conditions, by contrast, vary considerably over short periods—too quickly, in fact, to generate the intellectual frameworks necessary for interpreting them. Such frameworks are readily available from the ongoing influences of culture and religion. Not surprisingly, then, conflicts arising from cultural values are the permanent basis of electoral coalitions, waxing and waning in proportion to the power of short-term factors, such as economic conditions.

The neglect of cultural factors in the conventional understanding of American politics reflects in part the inadequate attention paid to religion in survey research. Surveys have measured religious affiliation —and thus religious tradition—very poorly over the years.[16] However, two recent innovations have improved surveys. First, new questions give respondents the option of indicating the *absence* of religious affiliation, thus reducing the temptation to mention a past affiliation or invent a present one. Second, new questions probe for more complete information; for example, they distinguish "Lutherans" and "Methodists" in more conservative denominations such as the Lutheran Church–Missouri Synod and the Free Methodist Church, from their Mainline cousins in such bodies as the Evangelical Lutheran Church in America and the United Methodist Church.

Careful analysis of beliefs, practices, and origins of specific denominations allows researchers to place members accurately in either the Mainline Protestant or the Evangelical Protestant tradition.[17] The 1992 National Election Survey, the source of information for this essay, benefited from these innovations.

ELECTORAL COALITIONS AND RELIGIOUS TRADITIONS

A useful place to begin is to compare the 1992 election results with those of 1988, to see whether changes in Bush's coalition led to his loss in 1992. **Table 1** (p. 48) breaks down the 1992 vote for Bush, Clinton, and Perot into three groups: those who voted Republican in 1988, those who voted Democratic in 1988, and new voters in 1992 (who did not or could not vote in 1988). The first column presents each category as a percentage of the total vote cast; these figures add up to the final election results of Bush 38 per cent, Clinton 43 per cent, and Perot 19 per cent. The second column gives each category as a percentage of the candidate's own total vote.[18]

In 1992, "standpat" Republicans, those who voted Republican in both 1988 and 1992, accounted for just over one-quarter of all the votes cast and better than two-thirds of Bush's total. "Standpat" Democrats (who voted Democratic in both elections) also accounted for about one-quarter of the total votes cast, but only about three-fifths of Clinton's total.

Both major-party candidates gained defectors from the other party's 1988 voters (for convenience we will use the terms "Republican defectors" and "Democratic defectors" to refer to those who voted for the party's candidate in 1988 but not in 1992). Clinton enjoyed an almost two-to-one advantage over Bush (7 to 4 per cent) in defectors. Clinton also did somewhat better than Bush in attracting new voters (10 to 8 per cent). Perot won more Republican defectors than did Clinton, and drew almost as many Democratic defectors. The second column of the table shows that more than two-fifths of Perot's votes came at Bush's expense (i.e., from Republican defectors) and less than one-third at Clinton's. Perot drew fewer new voters than the other candidates, but the new voters were slightly more important to him as a percentage of his total vote.

These figures help put the 1992 popular vote in perspective. Of the

TABLE 1

THE 1992 VOTE:
BY SOURCES
(As Percentage of Total Vote Cast and Candidate's Total Vote)

	Total Vote	Candidate's Vote
BUSH VOTE FROM:		
1988 Republicans	26%	69%
1988 Democrats	4	10
New Voters	8	21
Bush Subtotal	38%	100%
CLINTON VOTE FROM:		
1988 Republicans	7%	17%
1988 Democrats	26	60
New Voters	10	23
Clinton Subtotal	43%	100%
PEROT VOTE FROM:		
1988 Republicans	8%	42%
1988 Democrats	6	31
New Voters	5	26
Perot Subtotal	19%	100%
TOTAL	100%	—

Source: 1992 National Election Study, University of Michigan

total vote cast, Clinton gained 7 per cent in Republican defectors, but lost 4 per cent in Democratic defectors to Bush, for a net defectors' gain of 3 per cent—less than his 5 per cent popular-vote margin of victory; but when Clinton's advantage in new voters—10 per cent to Bush's 8 per cent—is added, the combination equals Clinton's 5 per cent margin. On the other hand, Republican defectors to Perot (8 per cent) were significantly larger than Clinton's margin of victory, and Perot also got 5 per cent from new voters. Bush lost the 1992 election,

TABLE 2

THE 1992 VOTE:
BY RELIGIOUS TRADITIONS
(As Percentage of Candidate's Total Vote)

	Evangelical	Mainline	Catholic	Secular	Others*	Total
BUSH VOTE						
Total Bush Vote	38%	24%	22%	11%	5%	100%
Sources:						
1988 Republicans	37	28	23	8	4	100
1988 Democrats	40	15	20	15	10	100
New Voters	42	16	18	18	6	100
CLINTON VOTE						
Total Clinton Vote	18%	17%	26%	18%	21%	100%
Sources:						
1988 Republicans	18	23	26	18	15	100
1988 Democrats	19	17	27	16	21	100
New Voters	14	14	22	25	25	100
PEROT VOTE						
Total Perot Vote	20%	26%	29%	19%	6%	100%
Sources:						
1988 Republicans	23	30	26	14	7	100
1988 Democrats	22	22	28	20	8	100
New Voters	12	22	35	27	4	100

*Other Traditions: Includes black Protestants, other smaller Christian denominations outside the major traditions, Jews, and other non-Christians.

Source: 1992 National Election Study, University of Michigan

then, because of a combination of defections from his 1988 coalition and the net impact of new voters.

How did the candidates' 1992 coalitions break down by religious tradition? **Table 2** lists the three largest traditions (Evangelical Protestants, Mainline Protestants, Catholics) plus Seculars and the Other Traditions grouping.[19] It shows both the percentage of the candidate's total vote and the percentage of each category of voters (1988 Republicans, 1988 Democrats, new voters) identified with each of these five groups.

Evangelicals were Bush's largest religious constituency in 1992, making up nearly two-fifths of his coalition, while Mainliners constituted one-quarter, Catholics one-fifth, Seculars and Other Traditions one-sixth each. More than one-third of the standpat Republicans were Evangelicals, and Bush's Democratic defectors and new voters included an even higher proportion of Evangelicals, with fewer Mainliners and Catholics.

Clinton's religious coalition was far more diverse, with Catholics accounting for more than one-quarter of his vote, Other Traditions (mainly black Protestants and Jews) about one-fifth, and Evangelicals, Mainliners, and Seculars less than one-fifth each. Republican defectors to Clinton included more Mainliners and Catholics, while his new voters were particularly rich in Seculars and Other Traditions.

Perot's coalition showed a similar diversity, with Catholics and Mainline Protestants accounting for more than one-quarter each, ahead of Evangelicals and Seculars, each at about one-fifth. As one might expect, Perot's Republican defectors included more Protestants, while his Democratic defectors were more often Catholics. His new voters were also heavily Catholic and Secular, so that Catholics were his largest religious constituency overall.

These patterns can be seen more clearly in **Table 3** (p. 51), which shows how the votes from religious traditions were distributed among the candidates. Table 3 presents the votes from each tradition for each candidate as a percentage of the total vote cast. In total, more than one-half of Evangelicals voted for Bush; more than one-third were standpat Republicans, while one-fifth were either Democratic defectors or new voters. Less than one-third of Evangelicals backed Clinton, and these were mostly drawn from standpat Democrats; only 5 per cent of Evangelicals who voted Republican in 1988 defected to Clinton, and another 5 per cent were found among his new voters. Perot garnered about one-sixth of the Evangelical vote; he drew modestly more Republican defectors than did Clinton, but these voters made up less than half of his Evangelical constituency: more came from the combination of Democratic defectors and new voters.

TABLE 3

RELIGIOUS TRADITIONS:
VOTE DISTRIBUTION IN 1992
(As Percentage of Total Vote Cast)

	Evangelical	Mainline	Catholic	Secular	Others*
BUSH VOTE FROM:					
1988 Republicans	37%	34%	24%	14%	6%
1988 Democrats	6	3	3	4	3
New Voters	13	6	6	9	4
Bush Subtotal	56%	43%	33%	27%	13%
CLINTON VOTE FROM:					
1988 Republicans	5%	8%	7%	7%	9%
1988 Democrats	19	20	28	26	46
New Voters	5	6	10	16	22
Clinton Subtotal	29%	34%	45%	49%	79%
PEROT VOTE FROM:					
1988 Republicans	7%	11%	8%	7%	4%
1988 Democrats	6	7	7	8	4
New Voters	2	5	7	8	2
Perot Subtotal	15%	23%	22%	23%	10%
TOTAL	100%	100%	100%	100%	100%

*Other Traditions: Includes black Protestants, smaller Christian denominations outside the major traditions, Jews, and other non-Christians.

Source: 1992 National Election Study, University of Michigan

Mainline Protestants and Catholics were almost mirror images in 1992. Better than two-fifths of the Mainliners backed Bush, while a slightly higher proportion of Catholics supported Clinton; Perot attracted more than one-fifth of each. Among both Mainliners and Catholics, Clinton made a modest gain over Bush with defectors and new voters, and Perot did even better. Seculars went solidly for Clinton, giving him almost one-half of their votes, with Bush and Perot roughly dividing the rest. Most of Clinton's Seculars were standpat Democrats, but new voters swelled their ranks. We suspect that Clinton's and Perot's Secular totals would increase if a more accurate measure of the Secular population were available. As expected, Clinton also did very well with Other Religious Traditions, receiving more than three-quarters of their votes, mostly among standpat Democrats but with an infusion of new voters also.

Religion mattered in other ways as well. An analysis of church attendance and other measures of religious commitment (basically, how seriously respondents take their faith) showed that Perot voters were drawn from the least committed members of each religious tradition, and that Clinton voters had lower levels of religious commitment than Bush voters. For example, among highly committed Evangelicals and highly committed Mainliners the vote for Bush was 70 per cent and 49 per cent respectively. Bush also broke even with Clinton among highly committed Catholics (40 per cent to Clinton's 39 per cent). Among highly committed members of Other Traditions, Bush's support was almost double his support in that category as a whole (22 to 13 per cent).[20]

Thus, despite the special circumstances in 1992, the historic religious underpinnings of electoral coalitions were quite evident. Bush held Evangelicals to a remarkable degree, adding to them a plurality of Mainliners and minorities of other groups, especially among those with strong religious commitments. Clinton had a more variegated coalition, with Catholics, members of Other Traditions, and Seculars playing leading roles, while Perot mobilized religiously disconnected Mainliners, Catholics, and Seculars. Bush's net losses among the last three groups were particularly serious. Although such changes from 1988 were smaller than many analysts seem to think, their pattern was consistent with the conventional wisdom. Our task now is to investigate the issue positions and priorities associated with these changes.

ISSUE POSITIONS AND PRIORITIES IN 1992

Americans were deeply divided over social issues in the 1992 campaign. For example, some 40 per cent of the public believed that abortions should be banned or substantially restricted, while another

45 per cent believed there should be few or no restrictions (with the rest falling somewhere between). Opinion on gay rights showed a similar split, with 38 per cent opposing and 37 per cent favoring. Attitudes on family values were, however, tilted to the right: 41 per cent strongly agreed that "this country would have many fewer problems if there were more emphasis on traditional family values," and only 29 per cent disagreed or held neutral views. For ease of presentation, we combined these three issues—abortion, gay rights, and family values—into a single index. When these issues were combined, some 39 per cent of the respondents held right-of-center views and some 30 per cent were left-of-center.[21]

In contrast to its polarization on social issues, the public was uniformly pessimistic about the economy. For example, 61 per cent strongly disapproved of President Bush's handling of the economy (only 20 per cent expressed any approval). In addition, 30 per cent of the public thought that federal economic policies had hurt them personally, and 35 per cent felt they were worse off financially. We combined these three measures into a single index, revealing sharply negative views of the economy: overall 69 per cent of the population held a negative assessment and 14 per cent a positive one.[22] Taken together, these economic evaluations amount to a devastating indictment of a sitting president.

What priority did the public give to these social and economic issues? Since citizens are likely to vote on the basis of things that concern them most, measuring *salience* is crucial to assessing the electoral impact of issues. Accordingly, we developed a measure of salience for both social and economic issues,[23] which we then combined with our opinion indices to produce a general description of issue positions and priorities in 1992.[24]

This combined measure reveals that social issues were dwarfed by economic concerns. Respondents giving priority to social issues were a distinct minority, accounting for only one-sixth of the sample; but among them, social-issue conservatives outnumbered liberals three to one (11 to 4 per cent). In contrast, those giving priority to economic conditions were nearly five times more numerous, at about two-thirds of the sample; among them, negative evaluations of the economy outnumbered positive assessments three to one (50 to 15 per cent). Another one-fifth had multiple priorities: 5 per cent and 6 per cent were social-issue conservatives with, respectively, positive and negative

TABLE 4

SOCIAL-ISSUE CONSERVATISM
AMONG 1992 VOTERS
(As Percentage of Candidate's Total Vote)

	Net Social-Issue Conservatism*	Net Salient Social-Issue Conservatism**
BUSH VOTE		
Total Bush Vote	+48%	+33%
Sources:		
1988 Republicans	+51	+37
1988 Democrats	+35	+25
New Voters	+44	+24
CLINTON VOTE		
Total Clinton Vote	-23%	-16%
Sources:		
1988 Republicans	-15	-10
1988 Democrats	-26	-10
New Voters	-21	-18
PEROT VOTE		
Total Perot Vote	+4%	+2%
Sources:		
1988 Republicans	+23	+16
1988 Democrats	-8	-8
New Voters	-12	-7
ENTIRE SAMPLE	+9%	+8%

First column: percentage of each category accounted for by net social-issue conservatives (+) and net social-issue liberals (-) (after liberal positions are subtracted from conservative ones).
**Second column:* same as first, but only for respondents for whom social issues were salient.

Source: 1992 National Election Study, University of Michigan

TABLE 5

NEGATIVE ECONOMIC EVALUATIONS
AMONG 1992 VOTERS
(As Percentage of Candidate's Total Vote)

	Net Negative Economic Evaluations*	Net Salient Negative Economic Evaluations**
BUSH VOTE		
Total Bush Vote	+13%	+4%
Sources:		
1988 Republicans	+35	+17
1988 Democrats	-75	-60
New Voters	-18	-9
CLINTON VOTE		
Total Clinton Vote	-88%	-81%
Sources:		
1988 Republicans	-85	-77
1988 Democrats	-94	-86
New Voters	-77	-72
PEROT VOTE		
Total Perot Vote	-69%	-61%
Sources:		
1988 Republicans	-53	-42
1988 Democrats	-83	-80
New Voters	-77	-65
ENTIRE SAMPLE	-55%	-39%

*First column: percentage of respondents with net negative (-) and net positive (+) economic evaluations (after positive evaluations are subtracted from negative ones).
**Second column: same as first, but only for respondents for whom economic issues were salient.

Source: 1992 National Election Study, University of Michigan views of the economy, while the remaining 1 per cent and 9 per cent were social-issue liberals with, respectively, positive and negative economic evaluations. These patterns are consistent with the results of network exit polls.[25]

Table 4 (p. 54) summarizes social-issue positions and priorities by categories of voters. For simplicity's sake, the table entries report "net social-issue conservatism," which we calculated by using our social-issue index and subtracting the percentage of liberal positions from the percentage of conservative positions for each category of voters (moderates were excluded). Thus, a positive number indicates a balance in favor of social-issue conservatism and a negative number reveals greater social-issue liberalism. The first column in Table 4 looks at social-issue positions overall, and the second column looks only at respondents to whom social issues were salient. The value of this presentation is that the balance of opinion in each category of voters can be seen at a glance.[26] Comparable figures for the Entire Sample, which includes non-voters, are presented at the bottom of the table.

These data reveal that, on balance, social-issue conservativism characterized Bush's coalition (+48 per cent). This was particularly true of standpat Republicans (+51 per cent), but markedly less so for Democratic defectors and new voters. In contrast, net social-issue liberalism characterized the Clinton coalition (-23 per cent), particularly among standpat Democrats and new voters. But note that Clinton's net social-issue liberals added up to only about one-half the proportion of Bush's net social-issue conservatives. Furthermore, Republican defectors to Clinton showed the least net liberalism. This pattern was even stronger for Perot's voters, who were on balance social-issue conservatives; the more conservative Republican defectors outnumbered the more liberal Democratic defectors and new voters.

Much the same pattern was evident once social-issue salience was taken into account (second column of Table 4), but with much smaller percentages, reflecting the overall lower salience of social issues. For both columns, the figures at the bottom for the Entire Sample help put these patterns in perspective: Bush's coalition was much more conservative and focused on social issues than the public as a whole, while Clinton's and Perot's coalitions were more moderate, more diverse, and less concerned with social issues than commonly realized.

What about economic evaluations? **Table 5** (p. 55) presents information on "net negative economic evaluations" and "net salient negative economic evaluations," calculated and presented in the same fashion as Table 4. The contrast with social issues is striking. On balance, Bush's coalition was characterized by modest net positive assessments of the economy (+13 per cent), but this tendency came exclusively from standpat Republicans, while Democratic defectors and new voters were quite negative. Clinton and Perot voters were even more pessimistic about the economy: about nine-tenths (-88 per cent) of the Clinton total and more than two-thirds (-69 per cent) of the Perot total held negative assessments. Clinton's standpat Democrats and Perot's Democratic defectors were the most negative, followed by their new voters, and then by their Republican defectors. The figures at the bottom for the Entire Sample reveal that Clinton and Perot voters were more negative on the economy than the public as a whole, while Bush voters were more positive—a classic division, with the large number of non-voters standing in between.

Table 6 (p. 58) offers estimates of the net impact on the vote of salient social-issue conservatism and salient negative economic evaluations, presented as a percentage of the total vote cast (as in Tables 1 and 3).[27] First, Bush gained more votes than he lost from salient social-issue conservatism. On balance, salient social-issue conservatives provided Bush with 12.5 per cent of the vote cast, almost twice as much as the 6.8 per cent Clinton gained from salient social-issue liberals; this gave Bush a minimum net advantage of 5.7 per cent. The bulk of both constituencies came from standpat partisans, which suggests that the social issues helped the major-party candidates hold existing constituencies. However, salient social-issue conservatives among Democratic defectors to Bush more than offset the analogous defectors to Clinton, and a similar pattern prevailed among new voters for Bush and Clinton.

Although Perot's coalition was on balance conservative on social issues, subtracting his salient social-issue liberals still leaves Bush with a 4.9 per cent net advantage. Overall, Bush received four out of five votes from those who had not voted Democratic in 1988 and for whom social issues were salient in 1992.

Just the opposite held for economic conditions. Bush gained very little from the economy (2.3 per cent of the vote cast) even among standpat Republicans; Democratic defectors and new voters did not

TABLE 6

NET IMPACT OF SALIENT SOCIAL-ISSUE CONSERVATISM AND
SALIENT NEGATIVE ECONOMIC EVALUATIONS ON 1992 VOTE

(As Percentage of Total Vote Cast)

	Net Salient Social-Issue Conservatism*	Net Salient Negative Economic Evaluations**
BUSH VOTE FROM:		
1988 Republicans	+9.6%	+5.4%
1988 Democrats	+.9	-2.1
New Voters	+2.0	-1.0
Bush Subtotal	+12.5%	+2.3%
CLINTON VOTE FROM:		
1988 Republicans	-.7%	-5.4%
1988 Democrats	-4.3	-22.0
New Voters	-1.8	-7.5
Clinton Subtotal	-6.8%	-34.9%
PEROT VOTE FROM:		
1988 Republicans	+1.2%	-3.4%
1988 Democrats	-.5	-5.2
New Voters	-.3	-3.0
Perot Subtotal	+.4%	-11.6%

*First column: + indicates net conservative and - indicates net liberal. *Both columns:* Entries use the same data as the second columns in Tables 4 and 5, but expressed as percentage of the total vote cast.
**Second column: - indicates net negative evaluation and + indicates net positive evaluation.

Source: 1992 National Election Study, University of Michigan

support him on this basis. On the other hand, Clinton enjoyed a net gain of 34.9 per cent of the vote cast on the basis of salient negative economic assessments, and Perot gained on balance 11.6 per cent. Even excluding 1988 Democratic voters, Bush secured only one out of six votes on the basis of economic evaluations. Indeed, net Republican defectors to Clinton on the basis of the economy more than equaled Clinton's popular-vote margin of victory. And, on the basis of the economy, new voters for Clinton and the combination of Perot's Republican defectors and new voters had similar magnitudes, each rivaling Bush's net gain from social issues.

It is worth noting that in 1992 there was a large reservoir of salient social-issue conservatives among non-voters, equal to 8 per cent of the votes actually cast. Some 53 per cent of this group expressed a preference for Bush, a figure that rises to 62 per cent for the two-thirds of these non-voters who were Evangelicals. Even average turnout among these non-voters could have made the popular vote very close. On the other hand, this group also had negative views on the economy. Perhaps cross-pressures between social and economic concerns helps explain their lack of participation. Overall, low turnout hurt both of the major-party coalitions in 1992: lower participation among Evangelicals hurt Bush, while similar patterns for Seculars and the Other Traditions hurt Clinton.

What role did religious traditions play in these patterns? As might be expected given our previous analysis, they provided the basis for the social-issue divisions and contributed to the economic ones as well. Evangelicals made up two-thirds of Bush's salient social-issue conservatives. While they were less common among standpat Republicans (55 per cent) and Democratic defectors (54 per cent), they were much more numerous among Bush's new voters (85 per cent). Evangelicals also accounted for nearly all of the salient social-issue conservatism among Clinton voters (particularly those who were standpat Democrats) and for more than one-third of analogous Perot voters. In contrast, Mainline Protestants and Catholics were divided ideologically as well as electorally, with each furnishing one-sixth of Bush's social-issue conservatives and almost one-third of comparable Perot voters, but also generating about one-fifth of Clinton's social-issue liberals. And at the other extreme, Seculars accounted for nearly one-half of Clinton's and Perot's salient social-issue liberals, particularly among Republican defectors. The Other Traditions also contributed one-fifth of Clinton's salient social-issue liberals, particularly among standpat Democrats and new voters.

Given the widespread economic pessimism of the electorate, it is not surprising that religious tradition was less important in shaping economic evaluations. But some differences are worth noting. Standpat Republican Evangelicals were by far the most positive on the economy, and Evangelicals in other categories were generally less pessimistic, followed by Mainliners, Catholics, Seculars, and the Other Traditions, in order of increasing pessimism. Careful statistical controls reveal that members of different religious traditions who had the same socio-economic status were likely to see economic conditions in quite different terms.[28] Thus, religious tradition influenced economic evaluations even when economic distress was at the forefront.

James Carville certainly had a point: the weak economy was crucial to George Bush's defeat and Bill Clinton's victory. But social issues helped keep the election relatively close. Evangelicals were central to this pattern and could have been more important if their turnout had been higher. A comparison of our estimates of the impact of salient social issues to the total Evangelical vote for Bush suggests the presence of important indirect effects through partisanship, group attachments, symbolic appeals, and candidate images. Traditionalists among Mainline Protestants and Catholics made a secondary contribution to the Bush coalition.

On balance, then, social issues helped Bush because conservatives on these issues were more numerous and gave them greater priority than their liberal counterparts. Although religious conservatives also tended to view the economy in a more positive light, they did not compensate for the defections from the GOP's traditional economic constituency.

THE CHRISTIAN RIGHT IN 1992

Thus far we have seen that Evangelical social-issue conservatives were an important constituency for George Bush in 1992, one that had been developing for some time.[29] Of course, the activities of the Christian Right were largely directed towards achieving this end, and we find some evidence that they may have helped mobilize Evangelical voters for the GOP. These findings are supported by reports of proprietary surveys conducted by conservative organizations after the election.[30]

A key element of Christian Right strategy in 1992 was **church-based mobilization** of Evangelicals, and the most important tactic was the distribution of voter guides through churches, sometimes by pastors and other church leaders and sometimes on the initiative of church members. These efforts were supplemented by the activities of local activists among their co-religionists and the messages of some clergy urging their congregations to vote. If these efforts were successful, we would expect Bush's social-issue Evangelical constituency to be characterized by regular church attendance (defined as attendance more than once a month).

By this measure, some 85 per cent of Bush's social-issue Evangelicals were regular church attenders. Evangelicals who voted for Clinton and Perot included fewer regular attenders (some 50 and 30 per cent, respectively), as did non-voting Evangelical social-issue conservatives (60 per cent). Similarly, in Bush's smaller social-issue constituency among Mainline Protestants and Catholics, 58 per cent and 80 per cent respectively were regular attenders, while others in their religious traditions attended church much less frequently.

Church-based mobilization was supplemented by **grass-roots efforts to contact voters** by direct mail and telephone banks. In many areas these activities blended with the get-out-the-vote and fund-raising programs of the Republican Party and with the campaigns of lower-level Republican candidates and conservatives running for non-partisan offices, such as school boards. If these efforts bore fruit, we would expect to find reports of a high rate of political contacts among Bush's social-issue Evangelicals. Here we use the broadest measure of voter contacts, including activities by parties, candidates, and other groups to mobilize activists and voters, even though we cannot tell for sure the precise source or purpose of these efforts.[31]

By this measure, 77 per cent of Bush's salient social-issue Evangelical constituency reported some kind of contact before the election, which compares quite favorably to the 45 per cent of all Evangelicals reporting contacts. Bush's salient social-issue conservatives in the Protestant Mainline reported an 81 per cent contact rate, compared to 61 per cent of all Mainliners, while the comparable Catholic group reported a 67 per cent contact rate, compared to 54 per cent for all Catholics. Interestingly, Evangelicals who voted for Clinton or Perot reported a similar contact rate (70 per cent), while non-voting Evangelicals reported much lower levels (35 per cent).

Even in Evangelical circles, many Christian Right organizations are controversial, and their effectiveness is related to their popularity. While we have no direct evidence testing such popularity, we do have a question asking respondents **how they felt about "Christian Fundamentalists**." It is not clear, of course, that the term refers only to the political movement, since "Christian Fundamentalists" are an identifiable social group, but the indiscriminate use of the term in election news reports suggests that it might. Positive evaluations among Bush's Evangelical supporters would suggest some influence by the movement.

Members of Bush's Evangelical social-issue constituency were quite positive in their evaluations of "Christian Fundamentalists," with 78 per cent giving them a high rating.[32] Their counterparts who voted for Clinton, voted for Perot, or did not vote had positive but considerably lower evaluations: only 50, 45, and 66 per cent, respectively, reporting a high rating. However, social-issue conservatives among Mainline Protestants and Catholics gave much lower evaluations: only 20 and 30 per cent, respectively, gave a high rating. And there was great antipathy to the term "Christian fundamentalists" among social-issue liberals of all sorts.

Finally, we also have some information on the **impact of the Republican National Convention** on vote choice. Given the negative press attention generated by the presence of Christian Right and other conservative leaders at the convention, we can try a modest test of the movement's detrimental effects on the Bush campaign. Some 6.6 per cent of voters reported making their decision right after the GOP Convention, with 4.3 per cent deciding to vote against Bush and 2.3 per cent deciding to support him. However, among these anti-Bush voters, 2.5 per cent were standpat Democratic voters, and most gave priority to economic issues. Only .6 per cent of the sample were salient social-issue liberals who did not support the Democrats in 1988, a figure equal to one-half of the 1.2 per cent of voters who were salient social-issue conservatives and supported Bush. The Republican Convention surely created tactical problems for the Bush campaign, but its measurable direct, negative impact on Bush's coalition was modest.

In sum, there is some evidence that Christian Right activists may have helped mobilized Evangelicals for Bush in 1992. This constituency was accessible through churches, reported extensive political contacts, and regarded the movement positively. On the other hand, the Christian Right failed to get a large segment of its potential constituency to the polls.

RELIGION AND ELECTORAL COALITIONS IN 1992

A myth should be discarded from the interpretations of the 1992 election: religious conservatives simply did not play the pernicious role in George Bush's defeat commonly assigned to them. Evangelicals are now an important Republican voting bloc, social-issue conservatism represents a source of Republican votes, and the Christian Right appears to be a modestly helpful ally.

Still, religious conservatives could well present the GOP with serious problems. Social-issue conservatism is simply not strong enough to be the sole basis for winning elections. If the polarization on these issues became fully salient, the net gains Bush enjoyed in 1992 could decline considerably. And although Evangelical voters are not yet fully mobilized, their numbers are finite. There are also strict limits to the helpfulness of the Christian Right—as media coverage of the 1992 Republican Convention attests.

The immediate repair of Republican fortunes requires a two-fold strategy First, **the GOP must carefully manage its coalition**: at the minimum, it must include all kinds of conservatives. Republican leaders should remember that Ronald Reagan's secret of coalition-building was a deft combination of economic, social, and foreign-policy conservatism. A major lesson from 1992 is that Republicans have some room to maneuver on social issues, with the prospect of benefits to balance against costs. Second, **the GOP must come to terms with the economy**. A broader repertoire of domestic policies and new ideas on economic management, particularly in hard times, is essential to building and maintaining winning coalitions. While neglecting the cultural underpinnings of the GOP coalition would be foolhardy, cultural allegiance alone is not a sufficient bulwark against poor economic conditions.

Since American politics routinely operates in the absence of all but the broadest consensus, different issue positions and priorities must be used to assemble enough voters to win elections. This is precisely how minority groups participate in the process of majority rule. The true test of such assemblages is not the comparison of any one element to the political mainstream, but whether the coalition itself can win and govern. And this insight does not apply just to religious conservatives, who, as we have seen, make up a sizable minority of the electorate. Jews, farmers, and gays are examples of much smaller groups that nonetheless have been important elements of successful coalitions. By the same token, neither victory nor defeat should be attributed to any one element in a coalition, no matter how controversial it may be.

If the GOP needs religious conservatives, the converse is true as well: Evangelicals, social-issue conservatives, and particularly the Christian Right need the Republican Party. Religious conservatives are most effective when they participate in a broader conservative coalition, and the Republican Party is the most accessible institution for this purpose. Becoming a partner in such a coalition is not easy: it requires equal measures of compromise, militancy, and sophistication. The move by some Christian Right leaders to extend the movement's agenda by taking positions on such matters as health care and NAFTA reveals all three features.[33]

In the long run, such activities may help create a new political alignment in the United States, where religious conservatives of all sorts would oppose religious liberals and seculars.[34] Such a development would place traditional religious values at the center of future Republican coalitions and would, ironically, reduce the distinctiveness and impact of the Christian Right.

Responses

1. Michael Barone

I agree that in American elections, cultural factors are more often important than economic factors. My college senior paper for the history department at Harvard was about midwestern election figures in the years 1890-1910. I found that instead of voting for Populists or Progressives, people voted for traditional parties or for ethnic candidates—Swedes or Germans in these cases. So far as I know, my research has held up.

I grew up in the 1950s in Michigan, which was perhaps the state with the closest thing to economic class-warfare politics. The rhetoric of politics and many of the coalitions were arrayed along the lines of labor versus management, United Auto Workers versus the Big Three auto companies. Labor-union loyalists would not think of voting for Republicans, and if you asked your rich friend's father what he thought of Governor Williams, a Democrat, you had to be prepared for seven minutes of uninterrupted invective.

But even in this economic class-warfare atmosphere, ethnic factors were important. The neighborhood in which I first remember living was about a third Catholic, a third Protestant, and a third Jewish. At the time I thought it was the typical American neighborhood, though I now realize that it would be difficult to find another elementary

---

Michael Barone is a senior writer for *U.S. News & World Report,* co-editor of *The Almanac of American Politics,* and author of *Our Country.*

school district with such a precise three-way split among the three major faiths. I must have been about six years old when I heard my parents say about the Catholics, "They all vote for the Democrats." I wondered why that would be true, and I've been pursuing the answer to questions like that ever since.

It makes sense that in America, cultural affiliations and cultural values that are clearly related to religious beliefs are more important than economics. In this country, economic status changes; people move up and down the economic ladder, over the generations and even within an individual lifetime. But cultural values tend to remain the same.

Remember Senator Joe Biden's borrowing of the Neil Kinnock line when he was running for the Democratic presidential nomination in 1987? Kinnock, head of Britain's Labour Party, grew up in a working-class area of Wales and told how his family had been downtrodden for hundreds of years and had never moved up on the economic scale. Well, it actually wasn't true about Joe Biden—his grandfather was a state senator—but even if it had been true, it wouldn't have sounded true to most Americans. Even Americans whose economic status is low for the most part reject the idea that they are stuck down there, that they will never be able to rise, that the rich people will never let them move up. That's not a picture of America that rings true to most Americans.

Religious and cultural attitudes do make a difference, and John Green and his colleagues have shown us that they made a difference in 1992. I reached the same conclusion by looking at the Voter Research Survey exit-poll data. The numbers for Clinton and Bush and Perot differed more by religious affiliation, by the indexes that the VRS had of strength of belief, than by any classification of economic status or occupation. This was a pretty clear indication of the importance of religion at the polls.

I am surprised by a couple of things in this paper and in some related things I have read. One is that very strong believers do not make up as large a percentage of the electorate as some rhetoric has suggested. I am also surprised to find out that we had a large and identifiable Evangelical vote thirty years ago, in the early 1960s, and that it was usually a Democratic bloc but withheld its votes from John Kennedy because of his Catholicism. In effect these voters were still fighting seventeenth-century religious wars, which continued until about November 1960. Then once a Catholic was elected and did not impose his religion on others, we all decided that it doesn't matter as much any more.

A third surprise to me was that the Mainline Protestants continued to vote Republican in 1992. Obviously they haven't been taking the statements of their church leaders as seriously as those leaders would like to think they have. It's a source of satisfaction to many of us that they seem to take the same approach to such things that Dan Quayle took to his college professors' liberal politics. These results tend to confirm my sense that Mainline Protestants are increasingly on the sideline.

The overall thesis that John Green and his colleagues present in this paper, that on balance the Religious Right issues helped George Bush rather than hurt him, I regard as persuasive. People who are strongly liberal on those issues are already committed Democrats. There's nothing much that the Republican Party can do to change them (except to engage in considerably more vote suppression than Ed Rollins was accused of doing). We do have to realize, however, that the liberal bloc is heavily over-represented in the public media, where, in a sort of wonderful Orwellian way, all the emphasis on diversity is producing a uniformity of belief. That is, diversity means that everyone believes the same thing.

Responses

2. Allen D. Hertzke

John Green makes a persuasive case for his central argument that the Evangelical constituency was a key voting bloc for George Bush. I would like to see more on how alliances might be built between that one quarter of the electorate and other segments. Where are the lines of possible coalitions? What are the impediments to such coalitions? I have a few comments to offer about the potential and the problems.

First, it would be helpful, I think, to clarify the term Religious Right. The term itself suggests the early 1980s fundamentalist resurgence—Jerry Falwell, Pat Robertson, and the like. When we talk about the Evangelical vote, we're actually talking about a distinct, though related, phenomenon. Evangelicals are not all members of what we think of as the Religious Right. Many Evangelicals do not count Robertson and Falwell among their leaders. They vote Republican for reasons other than mobilization by an organization. In fact, some of them are pretty much mainstream Republicans and were even hostile to the resurgence by Pat Robertson's group.

In a brief historical reference John Green says, "Throughout most of American history, what we call now Mainline Protestants have been

---

Allen D. Hertzke teaches political science at the University of Oklahoma, where he is also assistant director of the Carl Albert Congressional Research and Studies Center. He is the author of *Representing God in Washington: The Role of Religious Lobbies in the American Polity.*

the culturally dominant religious tradition." He goes on to suggest that "Mainline" somehow means accommodationist toward the world. While this is partially right, I don't think he has quite captured what recent scholars have suggested has in fact been the case throughout American history. For example, Methodists in the nineteenth century were Evangelicals; they were pietists. They were in the vanguard, in many cases, of Evangelical politics. Only when they became accommodationist toward the world did they begin to decline and become what we now think of as Mainline.

In *The Churching of America, 1776-1990,* Roger Finke and Rodney Stark present a bold argument that helps us understand this phenomenon. Using census data from the founding era throughout American history, they suggest that the Mainline is always in decline. Whatever has become the established, comfortable church in America will inevitably find itself on the downturn. Why? Because of the marketplace of American religion. Finke and Stark suggest that in this marketplace the churches that offer something different from the broader culture are the churches that will grow. Those that are comfortable with the world will decline.

I think Green slightly underplays the critical Catholic vote for Bill Clinton. He notes that compared to Bush's coalition "Clinton's coalition was far more diverse, with each of the five groups providing roughly one-fifth of his total." This oversimplifies a bit. The table breaks down Clinton's vote as 18 per cent Evangelical, 17 per cent Mainline, 18 per cent Secular, 21 per cent Other Traditions, and 26 per cent Catholic. There's a pretty big gap between 17 or 18 per cent and the Catholic 26 per cent. In 1988, Bush and Dukakis pretty much split the Catholic vote: the ABC exit polls gave the edge to Dukakis, the CBS exit polls gave it to Bush. But in 1992, Bush dropped from 50 per cent to 33 per cent of the Catholic vote, while Clinton and the Democrats retained a much higher percentage, going from 50 to 45 per cent. I think that Clinton's appeal to Catholics was an important part of his success. David Leege has noted that Bush didn't talk Catholic. This preppie, blueblood Episcopalian just didn't resonate with Catholics.

Regarding the short-term power of the economic factor: I was struck by the fact that different religious traditions seem to view the economy differently. I wonder why. Do we have any explanations for why some Evangelicals might view the economy more favorably than Mainline

Protestants or Catholics? Green also notes that there was a pretty sizable group of non-voting social conservatives who tended to be very pessimistic on the economy. It sounds to me like the classic cross-pressured voter. These people didn't know how to choose between Bill Clinton, who was too socially liberal, and George Bush, who had no answer to their economic discontent. You could say they were part of the long-standing American populist tradition, which to a certain extent blends economic progressivism and social conservatism.

A surprisingly large number of voters reported that they had been contacted and urged to vote. Of Bush's salient social-issue Evangelicals, 77 per cent reported being contacted before the election. And Bush's social-issue conservatives in the Protestant Mainline reported an 81 per cent contact rate. No doubt this meant Republican efforts in addition to Christian Coalition mobilization. So maybe we are wrong in thinking that party organization has declined to nothingness. There is some organization out there; masses of voters are actually being contacted.

John Green argues that contrary to the popular wisdom, Evangelicals helped George Bush immensely. However, if you go back to the distinction I made between the Religious Right and the broad Evangelical electorate, the second piece of the conventional wisdom—that the Republican Convention hurt the Republicans—actually finds some modest support in Green's analysis. The convention did seem to sway a small number of voters, a couple of percentage points, away from Bush. So both things can be true: that the Republican Convention hurt Bush among some voters, but that the mobilized Evangelical constituency helped him. A better handling of the convention could have helped George Bush, but so would a continued mobilization of Evangelicals.

Green suggests that there are limits to how far this mobilization can go, how broad the coalition can be. I think that many Catholics, even some socially conservative Catholics, are not entirely comfortable being a part of a coalition with Evangelicals. They still have some resistance to the Evangelical style of politics. Even if they have similar concerns about the family, violence in society, sex education, abortion, and other issues, Catholics, responding to Evangelicals, may say something like, "I can't stand those fundamentalists." And so coalition-building will still be tough, I think, between Evangelicals and Catholics.

I would have liked to see even more on black Evangelicals in this paper. We tend to think of the Religious Right as white, but of course blacks are heavily Evangelical in their orientation. Both Clyde Wilcox at Georgetown University and I have identified some sources of potential sympathy among blacks for certain parts of the religious conservative agenda. That would be the essence of coalition politics. But I wonder how far it could go. If Evangelicals were really successful in bringing blacks into the Republican Party, how comfortable would other Republicans be with that?

In summary, there is indeed some tough coalition work to be done by social conservatives who want to build an ecumenism of orthodoxy among white Evangelicals, Evangelical blacks, conservative Catholics, and conservative Mainline Protestants.

Comments

Michael Lienesch: If I were a Republican strategist, the immediate message I would get from John Green's analysis is that we don't have to worry about the Religious Right any more—they're locked into the Republican Party. If they voted for George Bush, they'll vote for anybody who gives them a wink and a nod. There aren't a lot of Evangelicals floating around in the Democratic Party, and there aren't a lot among the non-mobilized voters. The real constituency that the Republican Party has to go out and capture is the Perot vote. But these are people who are profoundly uninterested in conservative social issues. Therefore, to focus on social issues in the Republican Party is to condemn the party to permanent minority status.

John Green: The Republicans have indeed been fairly successful in mobilizing social-issue conservatives, particularly among Evangelicals. But constituencies do not necessarily stay mobilized; you have to work at them. Social-issue conservativism is not large enough to win national elections on its own, but on the other hand it's very unlikely that Republicans would win without it. So the neat trick is to take what Bush had in 1992—which was pretty minimal as a national Republican electorate—and then expand it by bringing back the Perot people.

This involves two things. One is running on a broad platform and

---

Note: These participants are identified on pages 117-18.

talking about the economy and foreign policy as well as social issues. Because of the differences in issue salience, the GOP really can bring disparate groups together; it's not an either/or proposition. And how do they keep people who don't necessarily agree with one another together in a coalition? By talking about different policies with different groups. For example, if a particular group of people are not excited enough about social issues to vote on that basis, then they're not likely to vote *against* these issues either if something else—say, their economic concerns—attracts them to the ticket.

The other key to expanding the Republican electorate is moderation. The GOP can approach social-issue conservatives by moving a little more toward the center, and also approach economic problems by moving a little more to the center.

To the extent that Republicans decide to make social issues the only platform they run on, they will have trouble. But to the extent that they abandon social issues, they will have trouble as well.

James Guth: It is very interesting to see what has taken place among Catholic voters, if you look at the Voter Research Survey and National Election Study polls from 1988 and 1992 and then look back into the past. You really do need to sort out different ethnic and racial traditions. Take white Catholics: what has happened in voting behavior and party affiliation is a very complex thing. In most of the elections in the 1970s and 1980s, the most observant Catholics tended to be the strongest Democrats. During the Reagan years, the Republicans made the biggest inroads among less observant Catholics. But these were the Catholics who deserted George Bush in 1992. They had been in the Reagan coalition because they tend to move with the economic winds, more than anything else.

But a growing number of conservative, churchgoing Catholics also are voting Republican and are beginning to identify themselves as Republican. In 1992, for the first time, the same patterns we see among Evangelical and Mainline Protestants appeared among churchgoing Catholics. They voted two or three percentage points more for George Bush than for Bill Clinton. If you break it down by age group, you see that younger observant Catholics are much more Republican while a lot of older observant Catholics are still sticking with the Democrats. We are beginning to see the same kind of division between the observant and the non-observant that we see among Evangelicals to some extent and even more among Mainline Protestants. The coalition of the orthodox may be extending itself from the Evangelical Protestant core through the Mainline and then into the Catholic tradition. Whether it will extend to blacks and to Jews remains to be seen. Certainly there is some evidence of a dynamic occurring here.

Robert Dugan: Allen Hertzke asked whether we had any explanations for why Evangelicals held a more favorable attitude toward the economic situation than other groups. I'd like to attempt a theological answer. It seems to me that for evangelicals you would read, not that they saw the economy more favorably, but that they saw it as less important. The principle enunciated by Jesus is, "Seek first the Kingdom of God, and His righteousness, and all these things will be added to you." When you have a candidate espousing what Bill Clinton did on homosexuality and the sanctity of life and other key moral issues, you have people who say, "Whatever the economic situation is, these other things are much more important." Those people accused Evangelicals who voted for Clinton of moral shortsightedness, or at least of selfishness for putting their own economic concerns ahead of far more important issues.

However, this constituency was not that well served by George Bush. His 56 per cent of the 1992 Evangelical vote, the figure that John Green offers in his paper, is a lot lower than what Bush and Quayle got in 1988: 81 per cent of the white Evangelical vote, according to the *New York Times* exit polls. Perhaps that reflects a decision by Bush that it would be better to be more politically correct than to offer strong moral leadership.

James Nuechterlein: John Green says in his paper that the Christian Right activities may help create "a new political alignment in the United States, where religious conservatives of all sorts would oppose religious liberals and seculars." Is there evidence that this is happening? James Davison Hunter in his book *Culture Wars* says that where in the old days it was Catholics versus Protestants, now there is a breakdown across denominational lines of traditionalists versus progressives. Can you make the Hunter argument fit with the evidence that highly committed people are more likely to vote conservative Republican? Is there a relationship between high commitment and a general cultural conservatism?

John Green: Yes, there is evidence in the mass electorate of this kind of polarization, a division based on religiosity or religious commitment rather than religious tradition. We saw it among activists and elites a long time ago. In 1992, despite all the other factors, the trend continued, and we think it's the wave of the future. How quickly it will develop is a really interesting question. Many of us expected that after Desert Storm Bush would be reelected and the major confrontation would come in 1996. Now, with the election of Bill Clinton, this new division may be even more evident in 1996.

Clyde Wilcox: I disagree with John Green's overall assessment of the net effect of social issues, the Christian Right, and the Republican Convention on Bush's general vote totals. Green looked only at those people who claimed to be motivated by these issues. This creates two problems. First, many of them are already committed to vote one way or another on the basis of other issues. Second, and more importantly, it ignores those voters for whom abortion (for example) is one of many considerations but is, as Rich Bond argues, "the straw that broke the camel's back." When I run the data with these factors taken into account, I find that the total effect of abortion, Christian Right figures, and the Republican Convention was a *loss* of 2 per cent for the Republicans.

Allen Hertzke: One point to keep in mind is that the number of people who are in some sense or another strongly religious is smaller than we have been led to believe by some Gallup surveys and other sources. If this ecumenism of orthodoxy takes place, it may involve less than half of the electorate; the number of people who take religion seriously may not be as high as 50 per cent.

Ralph Reed: There is a sense in which it is true that the only two constituencies that stayed with Bush were people making over $100,000 a year and self-identified Evangelicals. But what doesn't get talked about as much is the extent to which this was the greatest defeat for an incumbent president since Herbert Hoover lost to Franklin D. Roosevelt in 1932. And in that kind of electoral environment, a sinking tide lowers all boats. Bush's Evangelical vote dropped from 81 to 56 per cent. Those lost votes went to Perot, not Clinton; Clinton got the same percentage of the Evangelical vote that Michael Dukakis got. On the two Sundays before the election we distributed 40 million "Voter Guides," and our phone rang off the hook for days. Almost all the callers were people who were madder than wet hens about the way we described Perot in the voter guide. These were Evangelicals who had ruled Bush out, for whatever reason, and had decided to vote for Perot. They were very upset that we had listed Perot as pro-abortion and pro–gay rights. He was, of course, but he didn't talk about it very much.

I don't think that these Evangelicals were really drawn to Perot, or that they thought he was one of them or was deeply religious or held their views on social issues. I do think that by February or March a good bit of the electorate had ruled Bush out and decided he was not going to be reelected. A substantial chunk of our people, 17 per cent, then settled on Perot. When they got information about Perot that jolted them, they had nowhere to go, because they had ruled out Bush and certainly couldn't go to Clinton.

Richard Land: My impression is that Clinton did considerably better among Southern Baptists than among other Evangelicals. A lot more Southern Baptists went to Clinton than to Perot. The reason for that was not Clinton, but Al Gore. Gore is a much more exemplary Southern Baptist than the president. The Vietnam situation, which was a real problem for Clinton among Southern Baptists, was offset by Gore's being a Vietnam veteran. On other issues, too, Gore really helped the ticket among Southern Baptists. The choice of Gore was an exceptionally bold move, one that went against all the political wisdom: another white male, from the same section of the country, about the same age, and with the same religious affiliation. But it really did a lot for Clinton.

John Green: Southern Baptists as a whole, nationwide, voted just about like other Evangelicals. In Arkansas and Tennessee, where the Clinton and Gore ticket had a particular appeal, the Democrats did do a little better among Southern Baptists. Clinton and Gore ran a border-state campaign. They tried to cut the southern states out from under George Bush, while understanding that they already had a good shot at winning on both coasts. The border-state strategy helped not only in southern states but also in Ohio, Indiana, and Illinois. It was an inspired piece of politicking. Gore's religious background and his moderation on social issues helped implement this strategy. In addition, Gore was perceived as a serious person, in contrast to the popular perception of Dan Quayle.

Clarke Cochran: John Green in his paper mentions that maybe we have underestimated the percentage of Seculars. This is particularly so among the Catholics. A lot of people who are identified in the survey as Catholics are not closely connected with the church and really act more like Seculars. Do we have a good estimate of how large a voting group can legitimately be identified as Secular? And how does this fit into the scheme of coalitional politics?

John Green: Something like 3 per cent of the population claim to be atheists. Add another 4 per cent who don't use that term but who are clearly non-religious, and you arrive at the 7 per cent Secular found in most polls. If you probe very carefully, and allow people to say that religion isn't very important to them, and make it sound socially acceptable, then you get up to 15 per cent Secular. If you then add people who may have some residual denominational affiliation but don't have any other religious characteristics, the number goes up to 30 per cent Secular. Now that may be high. I certainly don't think you would go much beyond that. A good estimate for the Secular population, then, is somewhere between 15 and 30 per cent.

I think we can talk about Seculars as a cultural group. They are as united as Evangelicals on certain issues. On social issues they are very liberal, while on foreign policy and economic concerns they tend toward the left, but less than on social issues.

Michael Barone: I think the Secular group is growing. In the Times-Mirror election research, one of their groups was called Secular. That Secular group made up about 8-10 per cent of the electorate. They were very liberal on the cultural issues, somewhat mixed on the economic issues. They were called 1960s Democrats. In October 1988, when Bush was running the campaign against the Massachusetts furlough program and the other crackpot Dukakis issues, the Seculars moved away from Bush and toward Dukakis.

Seculars are almost polar opposites of the Religious Right constituency. What takes the place of religious belief in their lives is what I would call a sort of ideology of the inferior grad schools. In my experience as an observer of social policy, the schools of education, the schools of social work, are incubators of bad ideas—things like, "We'd have less crime if we had fewer people in jail." The Voter Research Survey data on 1992 showed that in many states, particularly in the coastal and northern states, grad-school graduates were more Democratic than people who were just college graduates. The grad-school people are oriented toward public-sector jobs. The belief system that takes the place of a religion in their lives is producing social policy on the ground. While the Republicans might pick up some of these people on economic issues, as they did in 1984 and 1988, the net gain will be small.

Marshall Wittman: It's my sense that the Clintons feel they have a spirituality gap with the electorate. In the last few months we have heard discussions of the politics of meaning, the president's favorable comments on Stephen Carter's book, even favorable things about Dan Quayle's Murphy Brown speech. If you are a Clinton strategist looking toward 1996, what do the 1992 numbers mean?

John Green: I would argue, first of all, that both major parties confront the same problem. The Secular population presents the same kind of problem for Bill Clinton that religious conservatives present for the Republicans.

The spirituality in the White House, whether it's sincere or not, is aimed at peeling back some of the social-issue conservatism on the right. I was struck during the 1992 campaign by how moderate Bill Clinton wanted to sound on social issues—not conservative, but very moderate. He came to Ohio on his famous bus trip and actually campaigned in a white Baptist church. Everybody was very impressed by him: here's this big liberal coming to talk to us. I think that this attempt to broaden the base through moderation on social issues is very important if the Democrats are trying to get to 50 per cent.

3

Talking the Talk: Christian Conviction and Democratic Etiquette

George Weigel

According to a bit of street wisdom that has worked its way into the national vocabulary, "You got to walk the walk, not just talk the talk." But the talking itself may not be as easy as we often think. As Christians in America, how do we talk the talk in such a way that moral judgments born of Christian religious conviction can be heard and considered by all Americans—or at least by those willing to concede that moral judgment plays a crucial role in the public-policy process?

The question of how Christians "talk the talk" in American public life will not go away, because it cannot go away; this is a fact of demographics, as well as a reflection of the nation's historic cultural core. For the foreseeable future the United States will remain at once a democracy, a deeply religious society, and a vibrantly, gloriously, and in some respects maddeningly diverse culture. And thus the 1990s will see a striking diversity of "vocabularies" in the American public square: many of them religious, others determinedly secular.

George Weigel is president of the Ethics and Public Policy Center and the author or editor of fourteen books on religion and public life. The most recent is *Idealism Without Illusions: U.S. Foreign Policy in the 1990s*.

This fact raises some important questions: Can Christians of diverse theological persuasions talk the talk with one another, as they deliberate their public responsibilities within the household of faith? And how can those diverse Christian communities contribute to a public moral discourse that sounds more like counterpoint than a cacophony? Finally, is there a grammar that can bring some discipline to the inevitably raucous public debate over how we ought to live together?

These perennial questions have been intensified over the past twenty years by two phenomena, distinct in their provenance but related in their public consequences.

The first is the return of conservative, evangelical, and fundamentalist Protestants to the public square. For decades they had been in the cultural hinterlands, consigned (and, often, self-consigned) there in the aftermath of the 1925 Scopes Trial and the modernist-fundamentalist fracture that culminated in the division of the Princeton Seminary faculty in 1929. For almost fifty years after that great trek to the margins of the public discourse, these conservative Protestants were content to remain in their enclaves, worshipping their God and educating their children as they saw fit, asking only to be left alone by the larger society. Then in the late 1970s, the assault on Christian day schools by the Carter administration's Justice Department and IRS showed that the enclave strategy would no longer work, and the result was the defensive/offensive movement we have come to know as the "Religious New Right."[1] That this movement dramatically sharpened the debate over the place of Christian conviction in public discourse is a statement of the obvious that needs no elaboration here.

The return of the evangelicals and fundamentalists from cultural exile was paralleled in the 1980s by a new assertiveness on the part of Roman Catholics (and especially several prominent bishops). On issues like abortion, pornography, school choice, and the claims of the gay/lesbian/bisexual movement, Catholic bishops, activists, and intellectuals who insisted on acting like Catholics in public soon found themselves in heated confrontations with several of the key idea-shaping and values-transmitting institutions in our society: the prestige press, the academy, and the popular entertainment industry. Perhaps the high (or low) point was reached on November 26, 1989, when the *New York Times* solemnly warned Catholic bishops that their resistance to abortion-on-demand threatened the "truce of tolerance" by which Catholics were permitted to play a part in American public life. Even by *Times* standards, this was a high-water mark in *chutzpah*.

Thus two groups that had long eyed each other with suspicion (if not hostility) now found themselves in common cause on a host of fevered public issues. The American democracy was faced, yet again, with the question of how it could be *e pluribus unum* in fact as well as in theory. And American Christians were faced with the question of how they could bring their most deeply held convictions to bear on public life in ways that were faithful both to those convictions and to the canons of democratic civility. Since the United States remains, in Chesterton's famous phrase, a nation with the soul of a church, the two questions were not unrelated.

Mars Hill, Then and Now

So far as we know, the apostle Paul was not overly vexed about the public policy of Athens in the first century of the common era, but Paul's struggle to "translate" the Christian Gospel into terms that the Athenians could understand suggests that our issue has a venerable history. The apostle's invocation of the "unknown god" to the men gathered on the Areopagus was, of course, an evangelistic tactic aimed at the religious conversion of his audience. Acts does not suggest that Paul was concerned to reform deficit financing, health care, education, or defense appropriations in Greater Athens. But that evangelistic instinct to seek a language—a grammar, let us say—through which the Athenians could grasp (and be grasped by) the claims of the Gospel is one on which we might well reflect as we confront such decidedly secondary questions as deficit financing, health-care reform, education, and defense appropriations in the American Republic.

Paul was a man at home with at least two moral-intellectual "grammars": the Judaic "grammar" in which he had been rabbinically trained, and the Hellenistic "grammar" that dominated elite culture in the eastern Mediterranean at the time. No doubt Paul regarded the Judaic "grammar" as superior to the Hellenistic; but he did not hesitate to employ the latter in the service of the Gospel.

This grammatical ecumenicity, as we might call it, was memorably captured in Paul's familiar boast, "I have become all things to all men, that I might by all means save some" (I Cor. 9:22b). Again, the questions with which we are wrestling here are of considerably less consequence than the salvation of souls. But if, in such a grand cause, the apostle of the Gentiles could appeal to his audiences through language and images with which they were most familiar—if, to get down to cases, Paul could expropriate an Athenian idol as an instrument for breaking open the Gospel of Christ, the Son of the Living God—then perhaps it is incumbent upon us, working in the far less dramatic vineyards of public policy, to devise means of translating our religious convictions into language and images that can illuminate for all our fellow citizens the truths of how we ought to live together, as we have come to understand them through faith and reason.

There is danger in this, of course, and it should be squarely faced: Christians eager to be heard in the public square may, through an excess of grammatical ecumenicity, so dilute their message that the sharp edge of truth gets blunted. Flaccidity in the cause of a misconceived public ecumenicity has contributed to the decline of the academic study of religion in America, as it has the decline of mainline/oldline Protestantism and the marginalization of the National Council of Churches. Some would suggest that a similar disposition to excessive public "correctness"—as that set of attitudes is defined by the tastemakers of our society—has also misshaped certain interpretations of the Roman Catholic "consistent ethic of life."

Moreover, it can often seem as if our cultural moment demands confrontation rather than polite dialogue. When unborn human beings have less legal standing than an "endangered species" of bird in a national forest; when any configuration of "committed" consenting adults is considered in enlightened circles to constitute a "marriage"; when senior senators bloviate about "sexual harassment" in kindergarten while national illegitimacy rates approach 30 per cent of all births: well, it all seems to summon up Orwell's observation, two generations ago, that "we have now sunk to a depth at which the re-statement of the obvious is the first duty of intelligent men." There is no burking the fact that there are some hard home truths to be told, on the various Mars Hills of the American Republic, and the teller of those truths, even in a publicly accessible "grammar," is certain to bring down upon his head the odium of those committed to establishing the American Republic of the Imperial Autonomous Self. Under such circumstances, the old country saw that tells us we may as well get hung for a sheep as for a goat retains its salience.

The Good News

But the bad news is not all the news there is. For we may also see, in certain signs of these times, a new public recognition of the realities of religious conviction in America and a new willingness to concede a place for religiously based moral argument in the American public square.[2] The warm reception given Stephen L. Carter's 1993 critique of the secularism of our elite culture, our law, and our politics suggests that seeds first planted by Richard John Neuhaus in *The Naked Public Square* are beginning to flower, however variously or confusedly.[3] The broad bipartisan, ecumenical, and inter-religious support that made possible the passage of the Religious Freedom Restoration Act in 1993 is also a good sign (though it remains to be seen just how the creative minds on the federal bench will bend RFRA to their own agendas).

Then there is the fact that we have a president who, unlike his predecessor, is unabashedly public about his Christian faith, and who seems to understand that the engagement of differing religious convictions within the bond of democratic civility is good for America. True, President Clinton's actions (and appointments) do not seem entirely congruent with his religious and moral rhetoric; and one ought not to dismiss as mere partisanship the suggestion that the rhetoric has been designed in part to divide the white evangelical vote and thus secure his reelection in 1996. But politicians will always be politicians, and those of us who take the bully pulpit seriously can still applaud the fact that the president of the United States publicly acknowledges that "we are a people of faith" and that "religion helps to give our people the character without which a democracy cannot survive."[4] However wide the chasm between the president's talk and his administration's walk, it is surely a good thing that President Clinton is not afraid to use religious language in public.

At the very least, the president's public appeal to biblical religion ought to remind us just how far from our roots we have strayed. In a nation whose coinage and currency contain the motto "In God We Trust"; whose Supreme Court sessions open with the plea (ever more poignant in recent years) "God save this honorable court"; whose houses of Congress begin their daily work with prayer; whose presidents have, without exception, invoked the blessing of God in their inaugural addresses—in a country like this, it should be the proponents of established secularism who are on the historical, cultural, constitutional, and moral defensive, not those who wish to bring religiously based moral convictions into public life. If President Clinton's use of explicitly religious language does no more than make clear who ought to be prosecuting and who defending in this matter of religion and public life, then the president will have done the country a good service, indeed.

Father Abraham

Still, having one highly visible exemplar of religiously based public moral argument does not solve our problem, any more than the remarkable popularity of the film *The Age of Innocence,* with its celebration of the superiority of marital fidelity over extramarital sexual passion, has solved the problem of the sexual revolution. What we may have today, through a confluence of forces (and not least because the crisis of the urban underclass has finally gotten the elite culture focused on problems of moral formation), is an opening through which we can begin the slow, laborious process of reclothing the naked public square. That the square has been systematically denuded, and that this has been bad for the country, is now widely acknowledged (save in some tenured bunkers where cultural vandals make merry while the cities burn and children shoot children over basketball shoes). The question now is how, and in what livery, it will be reclothed.

We have an important historical model for this, I think, in Abraham Lincoln's Second Inaugural Address. Here, as every school child used to know, Lincoln interpreted the national agony of civil war in explicitly biblical terms, citing Matthew's Gospel ("Woe unto the world because of offences! for it must needs be that offences come; but woe to that man by whom the offence cometh!") and the Psalmist ("the judgments of the Lord are true and righteous altogether") to buttress his general claim that the working-out of the American democratic experiment was caught up in a divinely ordered plan for human history.

But can anyone reasonably argue that, in his deliberate choice of biblical language and in his appeal to the notion of a providential purpose in history, Lincoln was being a sectarian? That his citations from Matthew 18 and Psalm 19 excluded anyone from the public debate over the meaning and purpose of the War Between the States? That his attempt to prepare the United States for reconciliation by offering a biblically based moral interpretation of the recent national experience constituted an unconstitutional "imposition" of beliefs and values on others?[5]

We recognize Lincoln's Second Inaugural as perhaps the greatest speech in American history precisely because, with singular eloquence and at a moment of unparalleled national trauma, it spoke to the entire country in an idiom that the entire country could understand. No one was excluded by Lincoln's use of biblical language and imagery; all were included in the great moral drama whose meaning the president was trying to fix in the national consciousness. Now, it is true that, even amidst the Civil War, the United States (north and south) was a more culturally coherent nation than the America of today; and certainly no statesman of Lincoln's eloquence and moral imagination is to be found in our current public life. Yet there still seems to be an important lesson here: that biblical language and imagery in public discourse ought to be used, not to divide but to unite, not to finish off an opponent with a rhetorical *coup de grâce* but to call him (and all of us) to a deeper reflection on the promise and perils of the American democratic experiment.

As the Second Inaugural amply attests, this principle does not preclude hard truth-telling. But Lincoln spoke as one who understood the frailty of all things human, and especially of all things political; he did not suggest, even amidst a civil war, that all righteousness lay on one side and all evil on the other; he knew and acknowledged that the nation was under judgment; and he spoke, not as a Republican and not as a northerner, but as an American seeking to reach out to other Americans across chasms at least as broad and deep as any that divide us today.

Such an approach—in which Christian conviction speaks *through* and *to* the plurality of our national life, so that *plurality* can become a genuine *pluralism*—ought to commend itself to us, first and foremost, on Christian theological, indeed doctrinal, grounds.

The treasure of the Gospel has been entrusted to the earthen vessels of our humanity for the salvation of the world, not for the securing of partisan advantage. We debase the Gospel and we debase the Body of Christ (which witnesses in history to God's saving work in Christ) when we use the Gospel as a partisan trump card. Our first loyalty—

our overriding loyalty—is to God in Christ, in the power of the Holy Spirit. Because of that loyalty, Christians in any *polis* in which they find themselves are "resident aliens," as the second-century "Letter to Diognetus" puts it. But this should help rather than hinder their contribution to the working-out of the American democratic experiment, one that has understood itself from the outset to be an experiment in limited government, judged by transcendent moral norms, and open to the participation of all men and women who believe certain "self-evident" truths about human persons and human community. The experiment could fail; it requires a virtuous people to succeed.

All this was implied in the Second Inaugural, and that helps explain the enduring power of Lincoln's address. None of us is Lincoln. But everything we say and do in public should make clear that our purposes are to reunite America through what Lincoln called "a new birth of freedom," not simply to throw their rascals out and get our rascals in.

There are also practical considerations here. Playing the Gospel as a trump card is not only offensive to Jews, Muslims, Buddhists, and secularists; it is also offensive to other Christians, even (perhaps especially) to those Christians who may be otherwise inclined to make common cause on public-policy issues. In brief, playing the Gospel as a trump card makes us less effective witnesses to the truths we hold about the way in which we ought to live together. Moreover, and to go back to our primary concern, the suggestion that Christian orthodoxy yields a single answer to virtually every contested issue of public policy is an offense, not simply against political common sense, but against Christian orthodoxy.

The "Natural" Thing

Lincoln's Second Inaugural, and its unchallenged position in the pantheon of American public rhetoric, ought to have secured a place for biblical language and imagery in our public life, the frettings of radical secularists notwithstanding. But, having seen in Lincoln a model for the proper deployment of explicitly biblical language in American public discourse, perhaps we should think for a moment about natural law.

This is not the place to explore the differences among the various

natural-law theories, or the points of tangency and distinction between Roman Catholic natural-law theory and Calvinist concepts of
common grace. Rather, the question before us is, How may Christians contribute to the evolution of a genuine *pluralism* out of the
plurality of vocabularies in American public moral discourse today?
How can today's cannonading be transformed, in John Courtney
Murray's pungent phrase, into a situation of "creeds at war, intelligibly."[6] The issue is a serious one, for society will descend into a
different kind of war, Hobbes's dread war of "all against all," unless
we can talk to one another and make sense to one another—or at
least enough sense to conduct the public argument that is the life-
blood of a democracy.

"Natural law" here means the claim that, even under the conditions
of the Fall, there is a moral logic built into the world and into us, a
logic that reasonable men and women can grasp by disciplined reflection on the dynamics of human action. The grasping of that logic may
be (and Christians would say, most certainly is) aided by the effects
of grace at work in human hearts; and the Gospel may draw out of
the natural law certain behavioral implications that are not so readily
discernible otherwise. But that such a moral logic exists, that it is
available to all human beings through rational reflection, and that it
can be intelligibly argued in public is, I think, a matter of moral
common sense.

We saw that logic at work in the American public debate over
possible U.S. military action in the Persian Gulf, in the months between Iraq's invasion of Kuwait and the beginning of Operation
Desert Storm. From one end of the country to the other, and in venues
ranging from radio talk shows to taxicabs to barber shops to bars to
the halls of Congress, men and women instinctively argued in the
natural-law categories of the just-war tradition in order to debate
America's responsibilities in the Gulf: Was ours a just cause? Who
could properly authorize the use of force? Did we have a reasonable
chance of success? Was military action a last resort? How could innocent civilian lives be protected? The country did not instinctively
reach for these questions because the just-war tradition had been
effectively catechized in our schools over the past generation (alas);
rather, we asked those questions because they are the "natural" ones
that any morally reflective person will ask when contemplating the
use of lethal force for the common good. Moreover, the rather high

level of public moral argument over the Gulf crisis (perhaps the highest since a similar "natural law" argument had been publicly engaged during the debate over the 1964 Civil Rights Act) suggested that this instinctive moral logic—the "natural law"—has the (perhaps unique) capacity to bring grammatical order to the deliberations of a diverse society. That is, it may enable us to transform *plurality* into *pluralism*.

To commend the development of the skills necessary for conducting public debate according to the grammar of the natural law is not to deny explicitly Christian (or Jewish, Muslim, or Buddhist) moral discourse a place in the American public square. All Americans have the right to bring their most deeply held convictions into play in our common life: that is (well, ought to be) the commonly accepted meaning of the First Amendment's guarantee of "free exercise." But the convictions most readily engaged will be those that are "translated" into a vocabulary that the hearers can grasp, and here the natural-law tradition can be very helpful. Two examples will illustrate the point.

The abortion license created by the Supreme Court in 1973 remains the single most bitterly contested issue in American public life. I take it as self-evident that Christian orthodoxy regards elective abortion as a grave moral evil, a profound offense against the entire structure of Christian morals. The steady proclamation of that truth, in love, has been a crucial factor in the perdurance of the right-to-life movement over the past generation. The overwhelming majority of those active on behalf of the right-to-life of the unborn are committed to that truth, and have remained committed despite fierce opposition from the elite culture, because they understand that the Lord requires this of us.

But how are we to make our case to those who do not share that prior religious commitment, or to those Christians whose churches do not provide clear moral counsel on this issue? And how do we do that in a political/cultural/legal climate in which individual autonomy has been virtually absolutized?[7]

I believe we best make our case by using these arguments: that our defense of the right-to-life of the unborn is a defense of civil rights and of a generous, hospitable American democracy; that abortion-on-demand gravely damages the American democratic experiment by drastically constricting the community of the commonly protected; and that the private use of lethal violence against an innocent is an assault on the moral foundations of any just society. In short, I believe we best make our case for maximum feasible legal protection of the unborn by deploying natural-law arguments that "translate" our Christian moral convictions into a public idiom more powerful than the idiom of autonomy.[8]

A second example: orthodox Christian morality unambiguously holds that homosexual acts violate the structure of the divinely created form of love by which men and women are to express their sexuality in unitive and procreative responsibility; thus "homosexual marriage" is an oxymoron, and other proposals to grant homosexuality "equal protection" with heterosexuality are an offense against biblical morality—what many would call an abomination before the Lord.

But given the vast disarray wrought by the sexual revolution, the plurality of moral vocabularies in America, and the current confusions attending the Fourteenth Amendment's "equal protection" guarantee, I believe we make a more powerful case against the public-policy claims of the gay and lesbian insurgency by arguing on natural-law grounds: that it is in the very nature of governments to make discriminations; that the relevant question is whether any proposed discrimination is invidiously unjust; and that the legal preference given to heterosexual marriage is good for society because it strengthens the basic unit of society, the family, and because it is good for children. Given the enormous damage done to the urban underclass by the breakdown of family life, this is, alas, an easier argument to make today than it was twenty years ago; and as that damage becomes more indelibly impressed upon the national conscience, we may well find that natural-law-based appeals to public responsibility for the welfare of children and families give us a vocabulary superior in political potency to the rhetoric of autonomy.[9] There may be a new possibility of conservative-liberal coalition-building on precisely these grounds, facing precisely these issues.

Similar models of argumentation can be developed for other "social issues," including censorship, school choice, school curricula, sex education, and public health. In all these cases, it should be emphasized again, the goal is not to weaken the moral claims or judgments involved, but rather to "translate" them, through the grammar of natural law, into arguments that can be heard, engaged, and, ultimately, accepted by those who do not share our basic Christian commitment (and, perhaps, by some of the confused brethren who do).

The Habit of Democratic Etiquette

If patriotism is often the last refuge of scoundrels, then civility can be the last refuge of moral cowards. Moreover, as Mr. Dooley pointed out a while ago, "pollytics ain't beanbag." That enduring reality, and the gravity of the questions engaged in the American *Kulturkampf,* remind us that civility does not equal docility or "niceness."

But there is an important truth embedded in the habit of democratic etiquette: the truth that persuasion is better than coercion. Public moral argument is superior both morally and politically to violence.

All law is in some measure coercive. But one of the moral superiorities of democracy is that our inevitably coercive laws are defined by a process of persuasion, rather than by princely ukase or politburo decree. And why is this mode of law-making morally superior? Because it embodies four truths: that men and women are created with intelligence and free will, and thus as subjects, not merely objects, of power; that genuine authority is the right to command, not merely the power to coerce; that those who are called to obey and to bear burdens have first the right to be heard and to deliberate on whether a proposed burden is necessary for the common good; and that there is an inherent sense of justice in the people, by which they are empowered to pass judgment on how we ought to live together.[10]

Thus in observing, even as we refine, the rules of democratic etiquette, Christians are helping to give contemporary expression to certain moral understandings that have lain at the heart of the central political tradition of the West since that tradition first formed in Jerusalem, Athens, and Rome (to take symbolic reference points). And, not so inconsequentially, we are thereby taking a stand against the totalitarian temptation that lurks at the heart of every modern state, including every modern democratic state. That is not the most important "public" thing we do as Christians, but it is an important thing, nonetheless.

Two sets of obstacles make the transition from plurality to genuine pluralism in contemporary America even more difficult than it necessarily is.

The first obstacle is the legal and cultural sediment of the Supreme Court's First Amendment religion-clause jurisprudence over the past fifty years. There is neither time nor space here to review this sorry history in detail.[11] Suffice it to say that the Court's strange decision to divide what is clearly one religion clause into two "religion clauses," and its subsequent tortuous efforts to "balance" the claims of "free exercise" and "no establishment" through Rube Goldberg contraptions like the three-part *Lemon* test," have led the justices into a jurisprudential labyrinth of exceptional darkness and complexity. Worse, they have created a legal and cultural climate in which the public exercise of religious conviction is too often understood as a quirk to be tolerated rather than a fundamental human right that any just state is obliged to acknowledge. In sum, the justices' increasingly bizarre balancing act has elevated "no establishment" and subordinated "free exercise" to the point where a new establishment, the establishment of secularism, threatens the constitutional order. And until the First Amendment's religion clause is made whole again— until, that is, "no establishment" is understood as the means to the goal of "free exercise"—our law will remain profoundly confused and our political culture too often inhospitable to people of faith.[12]

Thus I cannot applaud Stephen Carter's suggestion that the answer to the "trivialization" of religious belief and practice in contemporary American law and politics is something like maximum feasible toleration for religion in public life. The free and public exercise of religious conviction is not to be "tolerated"—it is to be accepted, welcomed, indeed celebrated as the first of freedoms and the foundation of any meaningful scheme of human rights. And until we reverse, in law and in our popular legal-political culture, the inversion of the religion clause that the Court has effected since the *Everson* decision in 1947, the already difficult problem of bringing a measure of democratic order and civility into our public moral discourse will be endlessly exacerbated.

The second obstacle in the path to genuine pluralism is a certain lack of theological and political discipline on the part of the Religious Right.

Now this may seem a classic case of "blaming the victim." After all, in late 1993 we witnessed a campaign for lieutenant governor of Virginia in which the Democratic Party and much of the media portrayed the Republican candidate, an avowed Christian, as a high-tech Savonarola panting to impose a theocracy on the great Commonwealth, the Mother of Presidents, through such lurid policies as . . . well, school choice, informed consent prior to an elective abortion, parental notification of a minor's intention to seek an abortion, equalization of the state's personal income-tax exemption with that allowed by the federal government, tort reform, and a lid on state borrowing. Eight months earlier a *Washington Post* reporter had matter-of-factly described evangelicals as "largely poor, uneducated, and easy to command."[13] Of course, seven months previous to that the prestige press had batted nary an eye when Jesse Jackson, at the 1992 Democratic National Convention, told the Christmas story in such a way as to criticize those who would have objected to Mary's aborting Jesus. In these circumstances, in which fevered warnings are endlessly issued about the machinations of the Religious Right, and not a word is written or said about the agenda of the Religious Left (and its influence on no less powerful a personage than Hillary Rodham Clinton), it might seem strange to suggest that the challenge that must be raised to the establishment of secularism in America must be complemented by a call to increased self-discipline on the part of the Religious Right.[14] Yet that is what I think. And here is why I think it.

I think it first, and foremost, on theological grounds. A partisan Gospel is an ideological Gospel, and, as many of us insisted against the claims of liberation theology in the 1970s and 1980s, an ideologically driven Gospel is a debasement of the Gospel. "Christian scorecards" that suggest the Gospel provides a "Christian answer" to President Clinton's economic stimulus package, to the administration's tax proposals, to questions of voting rules in the House of Representatives, and to a raising of the federal debt ceiling demean the Gospel by identifying it with an ideological agenda.[15]

My second concern arises from democratic theory. I have no quarrel with describing our current circumstances as an American "culture war." But I would stoutly resist the suggestion, bruited by Patrick J. Buchanan at the 1992 Republican Convention, that a culture war is to be equated, willy-nilly, with a "religious war." The two are not the same. A culture war can be adjudicated, and a reasonable accommodation reached, through the processes (including electoral and juridical processes) of democratic persuasion; a "religious war" cannot.[16]

Moreover, the phrase "religious war" suggests that the answer to the issue at the heart of the culture war—the establishment of officially sanctioned secularism as the American democratic creed—is a sacred public square. But under the conditions of plurality that seem to be written into the script of history (by God, some of us would say), that cannot be the answer. Rather, the alternative to the establishment of secularism is the reconstitution of civil society in America, the achievement of a genuine pluralism in which creeds are "intelligibly in conflict." And genuine pluralism is not the avoidance of our deepest differences, but the engagement of those differences within the bond of democratic civility.

Any number of forces have declared war on the Religious Right. But the Religious Right should refuse to be distracted by that definition of the conflict, and should get on with the task of rebuilding civil society in America. Such a strategy is theologically appropriate and also, I suspect, very good politics.

My final reason for urging greater theological and political self-discipline on the Religious Right is that I think it just might win: thus it had better start thinking now about whether it wants to win as a force of reaction, or as a movement for the reconsecration of the American experiment. That choice will have a lot to do with how conservatives, evangelical Christian or otherwise, govern in the future.

When I say that the Religious Right just might win, I don't necessarily mean winning the 1996 presidential election, or the 1997 Virginia gubernatorial election, or the 1998 congressional elections. Nor do I mean to minimize the possibility that the current moral-cultural ills of America may lead to a kind of national implosion, perhaps in the next decade. That might yet happen, given the demographic realities and the sad state of our politics and our law.

Rather, I'm trying to express an intuition about the current correlation of forces in the debate over how we ought to live together. Irving Kristol was quite probably on to something when he argued that cultural conservatism is the wave of the future in the United States.[17] The secularization project, for all that it dominates the network airwaves and the academy, has largely failed; Americans are, arguably, *more* religious today than they were fifty years ago. And the growing ends of American religion are not the mainline/oldline churches that have given theological and moral acquiescence to the secularization project but the churches that make the most serious doctrinal and moral demands on their congregants. This, on the positive side, coupled with the undeniably disastrous effects of the sexual revolution, the welfare state, and the absolutization of individual autonomy, on the negative side, suggests that a revival of "traditional moral values" as the common ethical horizon of our public life in the late 1990s is not impossible, precisely because these values can provide a more powerful public idiom for confronting our problems than the thin, tired language of "autonomy."

In these circumstances, and to strengthen their position as a force for positive change and national renewal, the evangelical and fundamentalist components of the Religious Right are obligated to practice the public arts of grammatical ecumenicity: to learn how to "translate" religiously grounded moral claims into a public language and imagery capable of challenging the hegemony of what Mary Ann Glendon has styled "rights-talk."

For the cultural-conservative coalition that can revitalize American civil society and American politics will be a coalition that includes Christians of Protestant, Roman Catholic, and Orthodox commitment; Jews who have broken ranks with the reflexive secularism and lifestyle liberalism that have typically informed late-twentieth-century American Jewry's approach to the public square; a few secular people; and, just perhaps, a considerable number of Muslims. Grammatical ecumenicity *within* this coalition is essential to maintaining its strength in the cultural and political wars. And grammatical ecumenicity will be essential in exercising the authority of governance, so that the reconstitution of America as a nation *e pluribus unum* involves a deepening, rather than a theologically and democratically inappropriate narrowing, of the *unum*.

In talking the talk, in truth and in charity, with force and with wit, so that others can enter the great conversation over the "oughts" of our common life, the Religious Right can make a signal contribution to the reclothing of the naked public square in America. And in doing that, it will, I believe, be serving the Lord who stands in judgment on all the works of our hands, including our politics. For Christians, politics is, or ought to be, penultimate. Talking the talk in the terms suggested here helps keep politics in its place: and that, too, is no mean contribution to the reconstruction of civil society in America at the end of the twentieth century.

Responses

1. Michael Farris

I fully agree with George Weigel's central thesis and with almost all the details. I therefore feel that what I can contribute to the discussion is a few illustrations—mainly from my experience in running for office—to back up his points.

Persuasiveness has been defined as guiding your truths around another's mental roadblocks. Good language, well-chosen language, grounded in reason and logic, helps us do this. If instead we use language that *creates* such roadblocks, then we're not being very persuasive.

Several years ago I was seated next to a U.S. senator on a plane flying across the country, and we talked about, among other things, his views on abortion. He basically took the pro-choice view. I later wrote him to ask that he take the pro-life view on a particular bill that was coming up in Congress, basing my argument on what he had told me on the plane about his views on various issues. His reply to me said, "Of all the letters I've ever received about abortion, yours dealt most effectively with *my* views on the subject, rather than your own views." I didn't get his vote, but I felt I had had some success in opening him up to listen to me on other subjects.

In politics, our task is not only to do that on an individual basis but

---

Michael Farris is a constitutional lawyer and the president of the Home School Legal Defense Association. He was the Republican candidate for lieutenant governor of Virginia in 1993.

to try to do it with the public at large. We should try to convince people of the importance of our views according to *their* values, *their* language, the views *they* hold. You don't have the right to say, "Vote for me because of my views"; you do have the right to say, "Vote for me because your views and mine coincide." That was what I attempted to do in my campaign for lieutenant governor.

I agree completely with Weigel's comments about not using the Gospel or the Bible as a kind of political trump card. To do so is inappropriate, both politically and theologically. We're not going to vote on things that to me are crystal clear and non-debatable, such as the deity of Christ. To say to someone, "The Bible says so; therefore you need to agree," is appropriate only if that person accepts the Bible as the authority in his or her life and, moreover, has the same interpretation of Scripture that you do. That's a perfectly appropriate kind of discussion in our Sunday-school class: we have voluntarily bonded together, we hold a common theological view, and we can talk about public policy in the light of Scripture in that class. But for us to go outside and tell our neighbors to vote a particular way on the basis of a biblical teaching is totally inappropriate. Even within the Sunday-school class I must respect the fact that the person sitting next to me has as much right to interpret Scripture for himself as I do; even within the church we have to be careful about using Scripture as a "trump card" on political topics.

I am intrigued by Weigel's comments about using biblical illustrations in public discourse. The problem is, I think, that not many people will understand them. You cannot go out in public and talk about Uriah and expect that your hearers will know what you're talking about. The only sources of illustrations that are widely understood today are rock 'n' roll, sports, and television. You can tell stories about Joe Montana or Joe Gibbs or Tom Landry and be understood. Forget Uriah, David, Solomon, and maybe even Jonah unless you include the phrase "and the whale."

In the Tennessee *Mozert* case, the teacher's manual in the textbook series we were protesting said it is very important to study Greek mythology because, in literature, references to these stories are almost as common as references to the Bible. So the students were to study Greek mythology—but not a word about biblical literature, of course. Public education has not trained our children to understand the many, many illustrations and allusions in literature that come from Scripture.

If we cannot cite the Bible as a source of authority in the public square, is there any higher authority that most people would respect? Yes: the Constitution of the United States. Almost all Americans have a great reverence for the Constitution. If you can make your arguments in constitutional terms, people are likely to be inspired and to agree even if they don't understand the arguments fully. The Constitution is a source of higher authority that is basically non-controversial.

Having been the executive director of a state chapter of the Moral Majority, I'm very sensitive to the problem of organizational names. In Washington state, we changed our name to the Bill of Rights Legal Foundation. The left has an easier time with organizational names because of a double standard. "People for the American Way" is an arrogant name; it suggests that anyone not in sympathy with this group's aims is un-American. But People for the American Way hasn't been charged with arrogance. This militantly secular group is close to being the left's equivalent of the Ku Klux Klan. The very purpose of its formation was to oppose born-again Christians in politics. If a group of people said their purpose in organizing their group was to oppose, say, Lutherans and Jews in politics, they would be shunned as extremist religious bigots. But People for the American Way can parade around as religiously tolerant civil libertarians even though they are doing virtually the same thing, because they have chosen politically acceptable targets.

One more point, with all due respect to my colleague Ralph Reed: the Christian "Voter Guide" has a place, and that place is in the church, before the election. If you are going to use that terminology, please don't bring it out on election day. I was in polling places in Richmond, Virginia, where one or two sweet people were handing out these scorecards on election day. I wish I had had the courage to say to them, "Please throw those in the wastebasket," because I was losing votes with every one that was handed out. We cannot afford to bring something labeled "the Christian answer" into the secular political arena.

When I was interviewed by the *Washington Post* editorial board during the campaign, I walked in with no illusions at all of gaining their endorsement; I just hoped to tone down the vehemence of what I was sure they would say against me. I was asked whether I thought the United States was a Christian nation. My answer was, "No, not in the sense you mean it." The difference is the difference between culture and government. I think that in its culture the United States was founded as a Christian nation, but the idea of a "Christian government" is something I do not ascribe to people like Roger Williams or James Madison. We should not read too much into the founding fathers' references to America as a Christian nation; these references have more to do with culture than with government.

Christians have the right to participate in government, to participate in policy-making, on the same basis as all other citizens. But to suggest that our goal is to create the Kingdom of God through the workings of our government is neither historically correct nor theologically correct; and it certainly is not politically wise.

Responses

2. Richard Land

George Weigel has undertaken an ambitious response to the need to create a grammar of public-policy discourse for our times. In discussing his paper with some of my theologian colleagues, I was surprised at the depth of negative response I got from some, because of Weigel's appeal to natural-law theory. One of them sent me a copy of a chapter of Carl F. H. Henry's six-volume *God, Revelation and Authority,* a chapter whose title is "The Rejection of Natural Theology."[1] That's really a bad title for a chapter that basically talks about the insufficiency of natural theology or natural-law theory *by itself.* Evangelical Protestants do affirm natural law, as witnessed by Francis Turitan, John Calvin, Jonathan Edwards, Charles Hodge, and Martin Luther. Yet none of these theologians based his arguments, public or otherwise, upon a structure of natural law. Indeed, Edwards warned that "a sufficiency to see the reasonableness of these things when pointed out, is not the same thing as the sufficiency to find them out," which he would say could come only from biblical revelation.[2]

There is needless division that can be minimized if evangelical Protestants and Roman Catholics will engage in serious dialogue about the differing functions of Christians as individuals and organizations that are specifically Christian in witness, as distinguished from Chris-

---

Richard Land is executive director of the Christian Life Commission of the Southern Baptist Convention.

tians as individuals and organizations that seek general reform in society. There are critical differences between individual pastors or churches with a specifically Christian evangelistic, redemptive, and discipleship agenda, and organizations like the Ethics and Public Policy Center that are trying to affect society and its public policy in a far more general way.

There is a huge difference between what Pope John Paul II says and does and what William Bennett as a Catholic politician and public official says and does. The pope should employ explicitly, unapologetically Christian language. A Catholic politician like Bill Bennett has a great deal more latitude to talk to a "public" public as opposed to a "religious" public, and to do so in ways that will appeal to the kind of moral discourse based upon natural law that Weigel is advocating.

However, we need not fool ourselves into thinking that a natural-law apologetic for our moral world view would be a panacea. The reigning cultural elites are seldom moved by natural-law arguments; they find them just as offensive, when they can comprehend them, as they do appeals to special revelation, as illustrated by the Bork and Thomas hearings before the Senate Judiciary Committee. The reason, I think, is that we are facing a basically pagan culture, not one with, as Francis Schaeffer described it, a Christian memory. George Barna has shown that a significant majority of Americans—66 per cent of all adults in his 1991 survey—reject the very idea of absolute truth. And interestingly, 73 per cent of those who identified themselves as members of mainline Protestant denominations rejected any notion of absolute truth.[3] Their only absolute is that there are no absolutes. And so the collective moral imagination of the nation has now been transformed from a discussion of what is right and what is wrong to a discussion of your rights and my rights.

In Charles Colson's Templeton Prize address, "The Enduring Revolution," which I would recommend to all of you, he talks about the four horsemen of the modern apocalypse that ride across our land and sow devastation. The first horseman represents the myth of the goodness of man, which denies evil, thus multiplying its effect. The second horseman represents the myth of a coming utopia, the idea that human nature can be perfected by government, which has led to great agony and bloodshed in the twentieth century. The third horseman of the modern apocalypse represents the myth of the relativity of all moral values, which sows chaos and confusion. The fourth horseman is the myth of radical individualism, which dismisses family and church and country, denies any value of sacrifice, and wants to speak solely about self-actualization.[4]

Colson is devastatingly accurate in his assessment of society's current crisis. We need to understand the nature of what we confront. Appeals to the kind of discourse that George Weigel wants to construct can gain more hearing than we will get with the kind of explicit appeal to special revelation that more and more Americans find incomprehensible. However, there will be limits to its success, for we will bump up against the prevailing anti-theistic bias at various points. We will also have a great deal of convincing to do among our various religious publics in order to reconstruct Christian understandings, in order to begin to win a battle for public opinion. And public opinion is where it will be decided in our culture. Richard John Neuhaus drew attention to something Abraham Lincoln said in a debate with Stephen Douglas. "In this age and this country," Lincoln said, "public sentiment is everything. *With it* nothing can fail; *against it,* nothing can succeed. Whoever molds public sentiment, goes deeper than he who enacts statutes, or pronounces judicial decisions. He makes possible the enforcement of these, else impossible."[5] That was true when Lincoln said it, just before the Civil War, and I think it is even more profoundly true today.

I share some of Weigel's concern about Stephen Carter's use of the word "toleration" in *The Culture of Disbelief.* Mark Twain said that the difference between the right word and almost the right word is the difference between lightning and a lightning bug. Perhaps that is even more applicable to the right concept versus almost the right concept. Carter has almost the right concept when he talks about maximum toleration of religion in America. But that's the difference between lightning and a lightning bug. What we want is maximum acceptance, maximum acknowledgment, maximum accommodation, because our duties and responsibilities to God as we understand them are far too important to allow any mere secular government to impose upon them. What we demand is religious liberty, not mere toleration.

Separation of church and state was never meant to remove faith convictions from the public square. Roger Williams made himself most unpopular with the Puritan grandees of New England, not because he was denouncing the Church of England as not being a true church or the Puritan ministers as not being true ministers, which he was indeed doing, but because he said that the colonists didn't own their land, having gotten it by patent from the King rather than paying the Native Americans for it. Roger Williams, the supposed champion of separation of church and state, was up to his colonial eyeballs in what was certainly the most shameful episode of public policy in the first century of America's settlement of North America, namely, our treatment of Native Americans.

Stephen Carter's *The Culture of Disbelief* is receiving a hearing it would not otherwise receive in our society today because Carter, as a lawyer, is a priest (probably more accurately a bishop, since he teaches at Yale Law School) in our modern secular culture. The fact that he is also an African-American, an Episcopalian, and pro-choice only gives his book and its arguments greater impact. *The Culture of Disbelief* provides a tremendous opportunity for us to make our case for the right of people of faith to bring their convictions into the public arena. We need to write corrective reviews pointing out the errors and weak points in Carter's arguments, and to use the book's popularity as evidence that there have been systematic attempts to "sanitize" the public square of traditional religious perspectives.

We also need to talk seriously about the limits of public policy, what it can and cannot do. And we need to be clear about what we are trying to do in the public-policy arena. From our different religious perspectives, whether it's that of the pope in the Vatican or the Christian Life Commission in Nashville, a Baptist pastor preaching in a church or the U.S. Catholic Conference, our responsibility as expressly Christian organizations is to speak in expressly Christian terms. This is not true of individuals running for public office or groups that are seeking to build coalitions for public policy.

I think George Weigel is right when he says, "The suggestion that Christian orthodoxy yields a single answer to virtually every contested issue of public policy is an offense, not simply against political common sense, but against Christian . . . orthodoxy." The middle and the right wing of the Protestant Reformation have always been far more confident that there is "a Christian" answer or "the Christian" answer than the Reformation's left wing. I agree with Oliver Barclay's assessment in *The Intellect and Beyond* that there are Christian *perspectives* and Christian *views* and that there may be varying emphases on different issues. I do think there is a key distinction, in regard to what Weigel is encouraging us to do, between what Richard Land does as head of the Christian Life Commission and what Michael Farris does as a candidate for lieutenant governor of Virginia, between what the Vatican does when it issues an encyclical and what the Ethics and Public Policy Center is seeking to do in an entirely different realm.

Regarding the establishment clause and the free-exercise clause: these two clauses certainly cannot be totally separated, but there is a comma between them, one of the more important commas in American history.[6] As a Baptist I would argue from the free-church tradition that we do not want any entanglement of the institution of the state with the institution of the church. However, we must accommodate, acknowledge, accept, and understand the right of individual believers to the full "free exercise" of their religious convictions. For instance, if we are going to require our children to be on public-school property for most of their waking hours, for most of the months of their formative years, then they must be free to exercise the religious convictions that they bring with them from home and from church.

I personally don't think that Justice Kennedy's proposal of a "no coercion test" is an adequate substitute for the Supreme Court's so-called *Lemon* test. I don't think it safeguards enough against the appearance of endorsement. I would prefer to have an expansion of equal access and a clear understanding that students have a right to talk to students about their beliefs; this would emphasize religious pluralism, which is a basic value of our culture, rather than secularism. What we are practicing in our public schools today is a form of religious apartheid in which we seek to separate religion from the classroom and to provide an artificially secular environment that is totally distinct from the rest of America as we know it.

I have wrestled with the negative comments that some of my theological colleagues have made concerning the validity of natural law and what it is sufficient to do and not to do. Charles Colson has been very helpful to me in sorting out the distinctions between natural law and the explicitly Christian witness provided by propositional revelation. He pointed out in an article about "the pagan mind" that as late as the early 1960s, as many as 65 per cent of Americans believed the Bible and were more than passingly familiar with its contents. Today only 32 per cent accept the absolute veracity of Scripture.[7] Consequently, Christians today face a situation remarkably similar to the one that confronted first-century Christians, namely, a biblically illiterate and pagan culture. The Apostle Paul has given us the classic example of how to confront and to interact with such people. Appalled by the Athenians' idolatry, Paul first preached in the synagogue to the Jews. Then he ascended Mars Hill (Acts 17), using the altar to the "unknown god" as his point of departure and citing secular poetry before presenting the gospel message.

Colson used an example from his own experience of the progression from what may be known from natural law and natural revelation to the explicitly redemptive message of the Gospel. A reporter sought an opportunity to discuss religious matters with Colson. It soon became apparent that an explicitly biblical witness was incomprehensible to this reporter, and so Colson switched to a discussion of Woody Allen's *Crimes and Misdemeanors,* to *War and Peace,* and to C. S. Lewis's defense of natural law. Only then did the discussion progress to explicitly biblical material.[8]

Colson has illustrated the need to move from the connecting point between natural law and culture to an explicitly Christian witness:

> The world has changed, not through the militant dialectic of communism, but through the power of unarmed truth. It found revolution in the highest hopes of common men. Love of liberty steeled under the weight of tyranny; the path of the future was charted in prison cells.
>
> The revolution's symbolic movement was May Day 1990. Protesters followed the tanks, missiles, and troops rumbling across Red Square. One, a bearded Orthodox monk, darted under the reviewing stand where Gorbachev and other Soviet leaders stood. He thrust a huge crucifix into the air, shouting above the crowd, "Mikhail Sergeyevich! Christ is risen!"
>
> Gorbachev turned and walked off the platform.[9]

Much confusion and needless division can be avoided if we precede our discussion of the sufficiency and efficacy of natural law with our acknowledgment that, for evangelical Protestants, arguments grounded in natural law may suffice for public-policy consensus, but the right to explicitly biblical witness must be acknowledged as necessary for the Christian redemptive imperative.

Comments

George Weigel: Janet Smith from the University of Dallas offered a useful suggestion to another professor who had complained that eighteen-year-olds were already stewed in the juices of moral relativism. Ask them three questions, she said. "Is it ever okay to rape somebody? Can you discriminate against homosexuals? And should you ever park in a handicapped spot?" The odd thing about today's relativism is that it has thrown up its own absolutes. So we can play a bit of judo here. Right after the encyclical *Veritatis Splendor* came out I was debating a feminist theologian on the radio, and she said, "We live in the century of Einstein; relativity is everything. What do you mean by saying there are absolute truths?" I said, "Do you mean to tell me that in Birmingham, Alabama, in 1963, Dr. King simply had one vision of the truth while Bull Connor had another?" End of that particular sound bite.

I commend the reading of *Veritatis Splendor* because it's a very interesting blend of biblical and natural-law discourse. I also think it's the most important Christian moral statement of the last twenty years. It takes on every point that we have been discussing in regard to the roots of the cultural problem. But also, most strikingly for an authoritative document of the papal magisterium, it includes a moving meditation, extending over thirty some pages, on the dialogue between Jesus and the rich young man. This meditation begins with that young

---

Note: These participants are identified on pages 117-18.

man's question, "What must I do to have eternal life?," and explores
the biblical dialogue with great human sympathy and religious insight.
The pope then makes a rather densely argued natural-law case for
objective, normative moral truth. The encyclical ends by examining
the Christian pastoral implications of objective morality, and with a
striking reflection on martyrdom as, in a sense, the seal on our affirmation of and commitment to the truth.

Richard Land and I are going to have to agree to disagree on some
First Amendment stuff. He points to the pregnant comma, so to speak.
With our friend Richard Neuhaus, I like to point to the missing word.
Suppose that statement had read, "Congress shall make no law regarding the establishment of religion or *otherwise* prohibiting the free
exercise thereof." There is a single goal here, and it is free exercise.
We don't have two goals to juggle. As we've seen since *Everson,* when
the juggling begins, "no establishment" is absolutized and "free exercise" drops through the floorboards.

Erling Jorstad: Regarding the possibility that cultural conservatism
is the wave of the future and the secularization project has failed: I
think we need a fifth category, besides Mainline, Evangelical, Secular,
and Catholic—the Indifferent. I really don't see the main problem as
opposition from People for the American Way or the ACLU, but
rather massive indifference from the pagan culture. The polls say that
this is a religious country, and yet 40 per cent of the people don't know
who wrote the four gospels.

Michael Bauman: If Michael Barone is right that there is a growing
secularist bloc in America [page 77], and if it's also true that there is
a growing evangelical bloc, then that means there is a shrinking center.
Whether we like it or not we are probably poised for what some people
would call a culture war. I'm not sure that on the brink of a culture
war I'd like to counsel people toward a sort of cold-war rhetorical
détente with the other side. In the real Cold War, we didn't begin to
make substantial progress until the most powerful man on earth called
our opponent an evil empire. I think trying to make arguments based
on Acts 17 doesn't work. Paul's efforts there were unsuccessful; he
made no progress in Athens. When he spoke their language, he didn't
put us any further down the road.

The comments that are most successful today are those that are pointed, that are sharp, that are memorable, and that might make your opponent something of a laughingstock. Invective is to language what justice is to law: it's a way of giving things what they deserve. Sometimes you must call things by their real names whether you think it will be nicely received or not. We are dealing with a leftist movement that doesn't want to have a command of language but wants to command language. It wants to take your words away from you. That ought to be aggressively resisted.

Ours is not a deliberative society. If we think so, then we make the same mistake that John Stuart Mill made. Logical arguments don't very often win the day. We tend to vote on the basis of cultural affiliations; some of those may be susceptible to argument, but others are not. In such cases it takes rhetorical power and aggressiveness to mobilize people to rally around your cause. I just wonder whether this prudential rhetoric we've been talking about is going to be the rhetoric that does that.

Stephen Monsma: Chuck Colson has been pushing the concept of alternatives to incarceration for non-violent offenders. If Colson were to testify before a state legislative or congressional committee, I could see him making three different kinds of arguments. One could be economic: it's cheaper to have alternatives to incarceration, which costs, say, $25,000 a year. Second, he could make a natural-law argument, referring to the concepts of justice, restitution, balancing the wrong that was done. Or he could make more of a scriptural argument: look at the Mosaic law. What type of argument should he make? Which of the three is likely to be most effective before the committee?

Richard Land: Make all three arguments. Which one do you make first? In most situations, I might start with the moral argument, move to the economic argument, and then bring in the biblical argument. You get your foot in the door with what we have called the prudential argument, and then you have the ability to bring in the others. Martin Luther King was a Baptist preacher who cast his argument in biblical terms, but he also made a moral argument that extended way beyond people who were coming from a Christian perspective. The reason this strategy was far more successful in the South than in the North was that people in the South, though they had a very sub-biblical view of race and racial relations, understood his biblical language and were shamed by it. When he went north of the Mason-Dixon Line, it didn't work nearly as well.

Michael Farris: The issue is whether you even bring up the biblical argument. I think that, unless the circumstances were unusual, I would not make such an argument in public. If I knew that a particular member of the committee was a strong believer, then I would make that appeal to him privately. The pope needs to talk like a Christian, and Richard Land's Christian Life Commission needs to talk like a Christian. But when you are speaking in a general public forum, I think you make public-policy arguments on a broad base.

Clarke Cochran: Weigel's paper and the comments on it prod us to think more clearly about what kind of language is appropriate in particular communities of discourse. What struck me is that we don't extend this to our own religious communities. That is, we take it for granted that within the community we know what's right, we know what the biblical view is, and now we have to figure out how to talk to people outside. But it seems to me that we need to foster real discourse and genuine debate and dialogue within our religious communities also.

That's why I was disturbed by Michael Farris's comment that Christian scorecards are okay in the church on Sunday. I don't think they are. They are much too simplistic. They are not dialogue, they are not discussion, and they are not discourse. The idea that all Catholics or all Baptists would immediately agree with some list of issues is dangerous. If we cannot have discourse within the religious community, it will be very tough for us to have discourse outside it.

James Nuechterlein: Richard Land said that Protestants, including Luther, have affirmed natural law. It's true in a way. Luther talked about the Ten Commandments and said that those moral prescriptions are still binding on Christians. The rest of the laws, ceremonial and cleanliness laws, have been superseded by the new covenant in Jesus, but the Ten Commandments still bind us because they are an expression of natural law. I think that is a significant point. The social issues that get into the public square are often natural-law issues. Richard Land suggested that we never want to get to the position where we don't want to say, "Christ is risen." As a Christian, I believe that the most important thing I can say is that Christ is risen—when I am evangelizing. But there is very seldom an issue in the public square to which that is the appropriate answer.

Greg Jesson: Maybe a useful example of a natural-law type of argument would be the Sermon on the Mount. Christ there uses a type of argumentation that is not that much different from Aristotle's in the *Nicomachean Ethics,* where he asks, "What are the conditions under which human life flourishes?" He thought it was an empirical matter: one could go outside and look. Jesus argues that same way. Human life does not do very well immersed in hatred and anger. George Washington Carver said, "I will not allow another person to destroy my soul by causing me to hate him." In addressing sexuality, Jesus says: If you use other people as sexual objects, you are poisoning your own soul, and it will be impossible for you to love another human being. I find that people today are open to discussing issues of love and sexuality, the meaning of life, character, virtue. People know, whether they admit it or not, that their lives turn on these crucial issues.

Terry Eastland: I'm not persuaded that we can get either from natural law or from biblical imagery the kind of thoughts and words that will suffice within the American experiment. We have basically a rights-based country. Soon after Lincoln gave his Second Inaugural, in fact, the Fourteenth Amendment passed. It is part of the story of the explosion of the rights culture in the twentieth century. Basically what Michael Farris's candidacy represented, what Ralph Reed's group represents, is an assertion of a party of virtue as opposed to a party of rights. How do we bring about a virtue-oriented approach in a rights-oriented society? I'm not certain that a natural-law approach is adequate. There is another approach, the pragmatic approach, which says simply that a rights-based philosophy doesn't work very well, that rights-based liberalism cannot speak to current social ills.

Michael Farris: What we are trying to do is not to alienate people unnecessarily. Using decent, common language shows that you value your hearers as human beings and are not trying to run over them. I'm all for taking sharp views. I took sharp views in the campaign, but

I tried my best to use language that did not unnecessarily alienate people. The real key to political success is being able to translate high-level language into the people's language, to get them to think about life. If we don't have that ability, then we are fooling ourselves if we think we are going to have an impact.

Why the Nation Needs
the Religious Right

Fred Barnes

Three things about the Religious Right's influence on the 1992 election and in American politics are of particular interest to me. First, a myth that grew out of the 1992 Republican Convention in Houston; second, the surprising gains that the Religious Right has made, particularly in the media (National Public Radio presented a fair piece on efforts by the Religious Right to expand into the black and Hispanic communities); and third, the Religious Right's role in keeping alive moral issues and traditional values important to most Americans.

I was in Houston when the myth began. The Religious Right was said to have taken over the convention and to have imposed its own religious views on the Republican Party, with the goal of imposing them on the entire nation. The myth created a media consensus on the convention: that it was intolerant, mean-spirited, exclusive, judgmental, narrow-minded, or worse. When Pat Buchanan gave his speech, I happened to be sitting next to another Washington journalist who is a bellwether of press opinion. At first he loved Buchanan's speech, but two days later his view had changed entirely, as had the

---

Fred Barnes is a senior editor of *The New Republic,* where he covers politics and the White House.

view of many other press people. Now he felt the convention had turned into a hate fest because of its domination by the Religious Right. That became the conventional wisdom among reporters in Houston. No, they didn't conspire to reach this conclusion, but as they gathered to trade information and gossip, the consensus emerged that the Religious Right, if not in total control of the convention, at least had a large and pernicious influence there.

The evidence? It was the speeches by Religious Right people, like Pat Buchanan (even though he has little to do with the organized Religious Right). The mainstream press pointed to these speeches more than to the issues of homosexuality and family values. Pat Robertson's speech was cited. So was Marilyn Quayle's, though she didn't dwell on religious issues but talked about feminism and women who don't work.

There were 128 speeches at the convention, only three of which could be considered religious. Just one—Robertson's, which wasn't even given during prime time—could truly be called a Religious Right speech. Yet this was enough for the press to conclude that the Religious Right had dominated the convention.

A week after the convention, a TV producer—married, with one child—was still furious about Marilyn Quayle's speech, because the producer, a woman, felt it attacked women who work. Here's what Mrs. Quayle, who herself has sometimes worked full time, actually said: "I sometimes think that the liberals are always so angry because they believe the grandiose promises of the liberation movement. They are disappointed because most women do not want to be liberated from their essential natures as women. Most of us love being mothers and wives, which gives us a richness that few men and women get from professional accomplishments alone." This was hardly a broadside against women with full-time jobs. Nonetheless many women and men in the press took it that way.

In any case, the supposed domination of the GOP by the Religious Right didn't contribute heavily to George Bush's defeat in the November election. I think Bush was defeated because he signed the 1990 budget deal. Without that he would have been reelected. But in the media the view lingers that the convention was a critical moment that doomed Bush and his reelection chances.

The myth is not confined to the media. Spencer Abraham, the executive director of the House Republican campaign organization in

1992, ran for Republican National Chairman after the election and was defeated by Haley Barbour. Abraham talked to each of the 165 members of the Republican National Committee, because they were the electorate choosing the chairman. Amazingly, he found that a majority believed the press view of what happened at the convention, even though they themselves had been there and should have known better. Abraham was regarded as the Religious Right candidate, even though he wasn't.

Religious Right Gains

My second observation about the Religious Right is the good news that the fog hovering over it is beginning to lift. The hostility toward it has begun to soften. The 1993 races for Virginia governor, lieutenant governor, and attorney general greatly affected press opinion about the Religious Right. Since Virginia is right next door to Washington, D.C., the commercials for the races were on Washington television for national reporters to see. Clearly the Democrats overkilled in their attempts to discredit the Religious Right, trying to make it an issue not only against Michael Farris, a Religious Right favorite who was running for lieutenant governor, but also against George Allen, the Republican gubernatorial candidate. The Democrats cast Allen—who won—as a patsy for Pat Robertson, which he obviously is not.

The backlash in the press, while not sympathy, was the beginning of a recognition that the Religious Right is a legitimate bloc in the Republican coalition. I don't want to overstate this. But after talking to ten political reporters who followed the Virginia race—Christopher Matthews of the *San Francisco Examiner,* Gloria Borger of *U.S. News,* Brit Hume of ABC, Eleanor Clift of *Newsweek,* Carl Leubsdorf of the *Dallas Morning News,* Thomas DeFrank of *Newsweek,* syndicated columnist Robert Novak, Morton Kondracke of *Roll Call,* Paul West of the *Baltimore Sun,* and John Mushek of the *Boston Globe*—only two of whom are conservatives, I found that most agreed the Religious Right is not an evil juggernaut, as they'd previously thought, but rather is a viable element of the Republican Party. They acknowledged that during the campaign the issue of the Religious Right changed—from fear of a religious takeover to the unfairness of attacks on people for holding strong religious views. The result is a more positive view of the Religious Right, and that's a gain. The Religious Right has further enhanced its legitimacy with the secular press by tackling some non-religious issues, as in the Christian Coalition's decision to air TV ads critical of the Clinton health-care plan.

Moreover, there are other voices now arguing that religious views are a legitimate source of political values and should be included in the public debate. The political left doesn't accept this, insisting that religious people want to impose their views on everyone. But President Clinton dissents from that liberal view, and so does David Wilhelm, the Democratic National Chairman. When Wilhelm spoke to the Christian Coalition, he made a significant concession. He stressed that religious values are fine and legitimate as roots of political views. That's the Religious Right position. It is not the position of most Democrats.

Clinton and Wilhelm declared that people of strong faith should not be ostracized from the public square. Christians, Jews, Muslims, and members of other faiths can properly draw on spiritual teachings to guide their political views. Wilhelm has also noted, "Let us say that while religious motivation is appropriate, it is wrong to use religious authority to coerce support in the public arena."

The Religious Right's Importance

The third thing I find interesting about the Religious Right is the notion that it is driving people away from the GOP, that most Americans want a party based on serious economic and foreign policy issues, not those horrible social issues. Here the real issue is the Republican Party's strong stand against abortion. If you are part of the elite opinion stream—where it is socially unacceptable to be opposed to abortion—you'll get flak from friends and maybe your spouse for being associated with such a party.

Richard Nixon, in an interview by William Safire, gave his opinion on abortion: "The state should stay out—don't subsidize, and don't prohibit." This view, that abortion should be kept out of politics, is shared by many other Republican politicians. I think this shows they are ignorant as to the party's real base. They don't understand who grassroots Republicans are.

The Republican Party does not stand a chance of becoming a majority party in America or electing another president without the Religious Right. Vast numbers of Americans are alienated from the

Democratic Party, yet are leery of the Republican Party. What attracts them to the GOP is not supply-side economics or hawkishness on foreign policy but serious moral and social concerns. I understand the reluctance of millions of former Democrats to become Republicans —the thought of being a Republican makes even me wince. But the Religious Right's cluster of issues attracts many of them.

Abortion is an issue that helped George Bush in 1992 and certainly helped George Allen win the governorship of Virginia. Millions of people were also attracted to Republican candidates because they believe in a role for religion in American life. Others became sympathetic to Republicans because they care about, for instance, the injection of gay values into the mainstream of American opinion, or about moral relativism. Whether it's the kind of multi-culturalism that shows up in the Rainbow Curriculum in New York, or Outcomes-Based Education, only the Religious Right keeps all these values-issues alive. And the beneficiary is the Republican Party.

There used to be something called the New Right, but it doesn't exist anymore. Its leaders were people like Paul Weyrich (who said in 1985 that the only serious grassroots activity in the Republican Party was religiously based—which is even more true now), Richard Viguerie, and Howard Phillips. But the New Right is now gone, leaving only the Religious Right.

If the Religious Right is driven out of the Republican Party, I think values issues—abortion, the role of religion in public life, gay rights, and moral relativism—will all but vanish. It is religious people who keep them on the table. Their departure would cause the Republican Party's base to shrivel dramatically. Republican elites simply do not understand this. I worry when Ralph Reed says that the Christian Coalition is not going to concentrate on opposing abortion because abortion cannot be blocked; instead, they will talk about parental consent and about other important issues like tax cuts. In truth, the Religious Right needs to emphasize the issues that brought its people into politics in the first place—basically moral issues.

The Religious Right's issues are critical politically not only for the Republican Party but for everybody. They are more important than cutting the capital-gains tax rate or aiding the Bosnian Muslims. They involve the moral upbringing of our children, the character of our citizens and our leaders, the way we regard and treat religious faith and religious believers. If American politicians do not want to grapple with these moral issues, the overarching issues of our era, then what are they in office for? Not much. It is the Religious Right that forces these issues into the public debate. They are not coming from anywhere in the Democratic Party, or from elite sectors of the Republican Party.

I do not always agree with the positions of the Religious Right. I am not really concerned, for instance, whether a school-prayer amendment passes. I have also disagreed with their style, although under Ralph Reed it has gotten better. But I give them credit for forcing things onto the national agenda that are critical to the Republican Party and to the rest of us.

In 1989, when Ronald Reagan returned to California on Air Force One, he was asked what his greatest regret was after eight years as president. He said he regretted that he hadn't done more to restrict or end abortion in this country. If an entire party abandons that issue and other moral concerns and ostracizes from the party the people who want to raise those concerns, the regret will ultimately be felt by the entire nation.

APPENDIX

Conference Participants

Fred Barnes, senior editor, *The New Republic*.

Michael Barone, senior writer, *U.S. News & World Report*.

Stephen Bates, fellow, The Annenberg Washington Program.

Michael Bauman, professor of theology, Hillsdale College.

Clarke Cochran, professor of political science, Texas Tech University.

Michael Cromartie, senior fellow, Ethics and Public Policy Center.

E. J. Dionne, Jr., editorial writer and columnist, *Washington Post*.

Robert Dugan, director of public affairs, National Association of Evangelicals.

Terry Eastland, resident fellow, Ethics and Public Policy Center.

Michael Farris, president, Home School Legal Defense Association.

Michael Gerson, senior policy advisor to Jack Kemp, The Heritage Foundation.

John C. Green, director, Ray C. Bliss Institute of Applied Politics, University of Akron.

James L. Guth, professor of political science, Furman University.

Allen D. Hertzke, assistant director, Carl Albert Congressional Research and Studies Center, University of Oklahoma.

Michael Horowitz, senior fellow, The Manhattan Institute.

Greg Jesson, social research analyst, Focus on the Family.

Erling Jorstad, professor of history, Saint Olaf College.

Melanie Kirkpatrick, editorial page editor, *Wall Street Journal*.

Richard Land, executive director, Christian Life Commission, Southern Baptist Convention.

Michael Lienesch, professor of political science, University of North Carolina, Chapel Hill.

Leigh Ann Metzger, deputy director of communications, Republican National Committee.

Stephen Monsma, professor of political science, Pepperdine University.

Gustav Niebuhr, staff writer, *Washington Post*.

James Nuechterlein, editor, *First Things*.

Ralph E. Reed, Jr., executive director, Christian Coalition.

George Weigel, president, Ethics and Public Policy Center.

Clyde Wilcox, professor of government, Georgetown University.

Marshall Wittmann, director of legislative affairs, Christian Coalition.

Notes

CHAPTER 1
"What Do Religious Conservatives Really Want?"
RALPH E. REED, JR.

1. "Government Is Not God's Work," *New York Times,* August 29, 1993.

2. Randall Balmer, *The Oregonian,* February 27, 1993.

3. Michael Barone, *Washington Post,* October 28, 1993.

4. William Bennett, "Index of Leading Cultural Indicators" (Washington, D.C.: Heritage Foundation, 1993), 2-3.

5. National Center for Policy Analysis, "1992 Update: Why Crime Pays," December 8, 1992.

6. Daniel Patrick Moynihan, "Defining Deviancy Down," *The American Scholar* 61, no. 1 (Winter 1993).

7. Michael McManus, "Churches: Wedding Factories or Marriage Savers?," *National and International Religion Report* 7, no. 23 (Nov. 1, 1993).

8. Stephen L. Carter, *The Culture of Disbelief: How American Law and Politics Trivialize Religious Devotion* (New York: Basic Books, 1993), 10.

9. "Energized by Pulpit or Passion, the Public Is Calling," *Washington Post,* February 1, 1993.

10. "The Coming White Underclass," *Wall Street Journal,* October 29, 1993.

11. Lauch Faircloth, "Principles of Real Reform," *Congressional Record,* November 20, 1993, S16672.

12. George Gilder, *Men and Marriage* (Gretna, LA: Pelican Publishing, 1986), 65.

13. Joe Urschel, "Religion: Don't Breathe a Word About It," *USA Today,* November 30, 1993; Carter, *Culture of Disbelief,* 109-15.

14. Charles Krauthammer, "Defining Deviancy Up," *The New Republic,* November 22, 1993, 21.

15. "Executive Summary of Virginia Election Surveys," Marketing Research Institute, November 3, 1993.

Response by E. J. DIONNE, JR.

1. Stephen L. Carter, *The Culture of Disbelief* (New York: Basic Books, 1993).
2. Terry Eastland, "In Defense of Religious America," *Commentary,* June 1981, 45.
3. James Davison Hunter, *Culture Wars: The Struggle to Define America* (New York: Basic Books, 1991).
4. Glenn Tinder, "The Spirit of Freedom: To Live Attentively," in Richard John Neuhaus and George Weigel, eds., *Being Christian Today: An American Conversation* (Washington, D.C.: Ethics and Public Policy Center, 1992), 152-53.

Response by MICHAEL HOROWITZ

1. *Policy Review,* Fall 1987.
2. See, e.g., Ben Stein, *The View from Sunset Boulevard: America as Brought to You by the People Who Make Television* (New York: Basic Books, 1979), and Richard Grenier, *Capturing the Culture: Film, Art, and Politics* (Washington, D.C.: Ethics and Public Policy Center, 1991).
3. Novak divides the influential elements of American public life into political, economic, and moral-cultural sectors. He finds a fair balance of forces, and fair debate, in the first two sectors, but finds the increasingly powerful community that focuses on ideas and values highly one-sided. Conservatives tend to flee from debate in a world they regard as hopelessly biased against them and often rationalize their conduct by asking the Stalin "how many divisions does the Pope have?" question. Conservatives thereby lose influence in an America where moral credibility is critical and ideas have important political consequences.
4. *The Dream and the Nightmare: The Sixties' Legacy to the Underclass* (New York: Morrow, 1993).
5. *The Spirit of Democratic Capitalism* (New York: Simon and Schuster, 1982).
6. *On Character: Essays by James Q. Wilson* (Washington, D.C.: AEI Press, 1991).

CHAPTER 2

"Murphy Brown Revisited"

GREEN, GUTH, KELLSTEDT, SMIDT

1. Cf. Lipset, Seymour M., "The Significance of the 1992 Election," *PS* 46:7-16; and Nelson, Michael, *The Elections of 1992* (Washington, D.C.: Congressional Quarterly, 1993).
2. Cf. Ceaser, James, and Andrew Busch, *Upside Down and Inside Out: The 1992 Elections and American Politics* (Lanham, MD: Rowman and Littlefield, 1993).
3. Cf. Pomper, Gerald M., ed., *The Election of 1992: Reports and Interpretations* (Chatham, NJ: Chatham House, 1993).
4. Morin, Richard, "Wrong About the Religious Right," *Washington Post Weekly Edition,* November 1-7, 1993, 37.
5. The authors are grateful to the Inter-University Consortium for Political and Social Research for access to the 1992 National Election Study. All interpretations of these data are the authors' responsibility.

6. Cf. Kessel, John, *Presidential Campaign Politics: Coalition Strategies and Citizen Response* (Homewood, IL: Dorsey Press, 1980).

7. Seligman, Lester G., and Cary R. Covington, *The Coalitional Presidency* (Homewood, IL: Dorsey Press, 1989).

8. Arnold, Douglas, *The Logic of Congressional Action* (New Haven: Yale University Press, 1990), 40.

9. Cf. McCormick, Richard L., *Party, Period and Public Policy* (New York: Oxford University Press, 1986).

10. Cf. Noll, Mark A., ed., *Religion and American Politics* (New York: Oxford University Press, 1990).

11. Swierenga, Robert P., "Ethnocultural Political Behavior in the Mid-Nineteenth Century: Voting, Values, Culture," in Noll, ed., *Religion and American Politics,* 146-71.

12. The sizes of the religious traditions given in the text are those produced by the 1992 National Election Study. Another study with more extensive religious data also conducted in 1992 suggests that the NES data over-represent Mainline Protestants and under-represent Seculars (Kellstedt, Lyman A., John C. Green, James L. Guth, and Corwin E. Smidt, "Religious Voting Blocs in the 1992 Election: The Year of the Evangelical?," *Sociology of Religion* 55, forthcoming 1994.

For further information on the denominational composition of the religious traditions see Kellstedt, Lyman A., and John C. Green, "Knowing God's Many People," in David C. Leege and Lyman A. Kellstedt, eds., *Rediscovering the Religious Factor in American Politics* (Armonk, NY: M. E. Sharpe, 1993), 53-71.

13. 13. Cf. Guth, James L., and John C. Green, eds., *The Bible and the Ballot Box* (Boulder, CO: Westview Press, 1991).

14. Leege, David C., "Religion and Politics in Theoretical Perspective," in Leege and Kellstedt, eds., *Rediscovering the Religious Factor in American Politics,* 3-25.

15. Leege, David C., Joel A. Lieske, and Kenneth D. Wald, "Toward Cultural Theories of American Political Behavior: Religion, Ethnicity, Race, and Class Outlook," in William Crotty, ed., *Political Science: Looking to the Future* (Evanston, IL: Northwestern University Press, 1991), 3:193-238.

16. Kellstedt, Lyman A., "Religion, the Neglected Variable," in Leege and Kellstedt, eds., *Rediscovering the Religious Factor in American Politics,* 273-304.

17. Kellstedt and Green, "Knowing God's Many People."

18. Like most national election surveys, the 1992 NES over-represents voters in both 1992 and 1988. To correct for this problem, the data were weighted so that the number of voters equaled the known level of national turnout (55 per cent in 1992 and 50 per cent in 1988). Only one significant difference derived from the weighting process: Mainline Protestants were more supportive of Bush in the weighted data (43 to 39 per cent).

19. The Other Religious Traditions were combined because of the small number of cases. Most of these groups tend to vote Democratic, but some, such as Mormons, tend to vote Republican.

20. Cf. Kellstedt, Green, Guth, and Smidt, "Religious Voting Blocs in the 1992 Election."

21. The social-issue index was calculated as followed. First, we modified the basic abortion question (V3735) from a four- to a five-point scale by dividing the pro-choice response into a modest-restrictions option (using items V3737, V3739, and V3732)

and an unrestricted-choice option. Similarly, we constructed a five-point gay-rights scale from three items (V5923, V5924, and V5926). These two scales and the family-values question (V6117) were then summed and recoded into a five-point social-issue index.

22. The five-point economic-evaluation index was calculated by modifying a basic evaluation of Bush's handling of the economy (V3324) by assessments of the personal impact of government economic policies (V3332), personal finances (V3426), and prospects for the future (V3428). Because most people took indeterminant positions on the last three items, high and low responses were used to augment or mitigate evaluations of Bush's performance.

23. We generated issue salience by first recoding all the open-ended likes and dislikes of candidates and parties to isolate mentions of social issues and economic evaluations (V3402 to V3424, V3110 to V3144). Candidate-specific mentions were excluded. Likewise, we recoded the open-ended items on the most important problems facing the country (V5722, V5723, and V5724) to isolate social and economic responses. Mentions of foreign policy and other kinds of issues were excluded.

24. The salience measure was added to the social- and economic-issues indices to produce eight different combinations of salience and issue positions. The different social- and economic-issue categories behaved similarly, so we were able to simplify the presentation by treating together all respondents giving priority to social or economic issues.

25. Cf. Kellstedt, Green, Guth, and Smidt, "Religious Voting Blocs in the 1992 Election."

26. Another advantage of using net scores is that it subsumes some odd responses that complicate the presentation of the data, such as salient social-issue conservatives who voted for Clinton, apparently under the assumption that he was the more conservative candidate. Such responses may stem from voter ignorance and/or the candidate's ambivalence on the issues (cf. Abramowitz, Alan I., "It's Abortion, Stupid: Policy Voting in the 1992 Presidential Election," presented at the 1993 annual meeting of the American Political Science Association, Washington, D.C.). A more complex presentation of the data shows similar results.

27. Table 6 takes the same data as the second columns of Tables 4 and 5 and expresses it as a percentage of the total vote cast. For example, the +33 per cent net salient social-issue conservatism for Bush voters in Table 4 equals 12.5 per cent of the vote cast in Table 6.

27. Readers might reasonably assume that differences between religious traditions on economic and social issues reflect differences in education and income. However, once these factors are taken into account, differences on economic and social issues persist to a remarkable degree.

29. Smidt, Corwin E., "Evangelical Voting Patterns: 1976-1988," in Michael Cromartie, ed., No Longer Exiles: The Religious New Right in American Politics (Washington, D.C.: Ethics and Public Policy Center, 1993), 85-117.

30. Guth, James L., John C. Green, Lyman A. Kellstedt, and Corwin E. Smidt, "God's Own Party: Evangelicals and Republicans in the '92 Election," The Christian Century, February 16, 1993, 172-76.

31. We used all the NES contacting variables (V5801, V5803, V5808, V5811, V5813, V5820, V5821, V5824, V5827), which were combined into a dichotomous variable indicating no contact and any form of reported contact.

32. Closeness to "Christian Fundamentalists" was measured by a standard 100-degree "thermometer" scale (V5338), which was recoded into five equal parts. The top two fifths were considered a high rating.

33. Seib, Gerald F., "Christian Coalition Hopes to Expand by Taking Stands on Taxes, Crime, Health Care and NAFTA," *Wall Street Journal,* September 7, 1993, A16.

34. Cf. Kellstedt, Green, Guth, and Smidt, "Religious Voting Blocs in the 1992 Election"; and Green, John C., and James L. Guth, "The Bible and the Ballot Box: The Shape of Things to Come," in Guth and Green, eds., *The Bible and the Ballot Box,* 207-27.

CHAPTER 3

"Talking the Talk"

GEORGE WEIGEL

1. See Michael Cromartie, ed., *No Longer Exiles: The Religious New Right and American Politics* (Washington: Ethics and Public Policy Center, 1992), and Nathan Glazer, "Fundamentalists: A Defensive Offensive," in Richard John Neuhaus and Michael Cromartie, eds., *Piety and Politics: Evangelicals and Fundamentalists Confront the World* (Washington, D.C.: Ethics and Public Policy Center, 1987), pp. 245-58.

2. I realize that, for many of us, this is not a "concession" but an acknowledgment by the state of a prior right. But more on that later.

3. See Stephen L. Carter, *The Culture of Disbelief: How American Law and Politics Trivialize Religious Devotion* (New York: Basic Books, 1993), and Richard John Neuhaus, *The Naked Public Square: Religion and Democracy in America* (Grand Rapids: Eerdmans, 1984). For a thoughtful criticism of Carter, see Phillip E. Johnson, "The Swedish Syndrome," in *First Things* 38 (December 1993), 48-50; Neuhaus himself offers an appreciation of the public impact of the Carter book in the same issue of *First Things,* 66-68.

4. "Remarks by the President at Signing Ceremony for the Religious Freedom Restoration Act," November 16, 1993, pp. 3, 2. President Clinton's comments on this and other occasions are in sharp contrast to President Bush's evident discomfort in publicly acknowledging religious faith. The cultural differences between Kennebunkport Episcopalians and Little Rock Baptists may have something to do with this. But even Bush's most ardent admirers would have to concede that he was very afraid of the "religion issue," which he seemed to regard as an expression of that "right-wing agenda stuff" he reportedly deplored. Most memorably, during the 1988 primaries, Bush, asked to recall what he had thought about when he was floating alone in the Pacific after his plane had been shot down by the Japanese, replied, "Mom and Dad, about our country, about God and about the separation of church and state."

5. Well, come to think of it, yes: one can imagine the ACLU raising unshirted hell, were any contemporary president to attempt such an explication of current events. But that simply illustrates just how far off into the fever swamps the ACLU, along with fellow-traveling smaller fry like Americans United for the Separation of Church and State and the Baptist Joint Committee for Public Affairs, has drifted.

6. See John Courtney Murray, *We Hold These Truths: Catholic Reflections on the American Proposition* (New York: Doubleday Image Books, 1964).

7. On this point, see the joint opinion of Justices Anthony Kennedy, Sandra Day O'Connor, and David Souter in *Casey* v. *Planned Parenthood of Southeastern Pennsylvania*, 112 S.Ct. 2791, at 2807.

8. This natural-law case is, of course, further strengthened when Christians embody their commitments to the "least of these, my brethren" by supporting and making ever more widely available alternatives to abortion for women caught in the dilemma of unwanted pregnancy.

9. As above, the persuasiveness of these claims is amplified by our making clear our rejection of anti-homosexual violence. Rejection of the gay/lesbian movement's public-policy agenda should also be complemented, as in many cases it is, by active ministries of care for AIDS patients.

10. On these points, see Murray, *We Hold These Truths,* 43, 45. Pope John Paul II has described these foundational truths of a rightly ordered political community as expressions of the "subjectivity of society" (*Centesimus Annus,* #46).

11. For the relevant cases and discussion of their constitutional and political implications, see Terry Eastland, ed., *Religious Liberty in the Supreme Court: The Cases That Define the Debate Over Church and State* (Washington, D.C.: Ethics and Public Policy Center, 1993).

12. On all of this, see Richard John Neuhaus, "Genuine Pluralism and the Pfefferian Inversion," *This World* 24 (Winter 1989), 71-86, and "A New Order of Religious Freedom," *First Things* 20 (February 1992), 13-17.

13. See Howard Kurtz, "Evangelical Outrage," *Washington Post,* February 6, 1993.

14. Why, one wonders, has the fourth estate not deemed it of interest that Mrs. Clinton's pastor at Washington's Foundry United Methodist Church, the Rev. J. Philip Wogaman, has publicly argued that the collapse of the Soviet Union was not the result of the intrinsic failures of Marxist socialism, but of socialism's not being taken seriously enough? If Ronald Reagan's occasional speculations on the meaning of certain images in the Book of Revelation were legitimate grist for the journalistic mill, why aren't Dr. Wogaman's singular readings of contemporary history? (See "United Methodist Newscope," September 11, 1992, 2.)

15. As did the Fall 1993 Edition of the "Christian Coalition Congressional Scorecard." I share the concerns of the editors of *First Things,* when they wrote the following about the Christian Coalition:

> Christian is not just another word but the name by which those who profess Jesus Christ as Lord are named. "It was in Antioch that the disciples first received the name of Christians" (*Acts* 11). To claim the name for a partisan political faction is troubling. And it is even more troubling when the rhetoric of that faction suggests that who is and who is not a "true Christian" is defined by agreement with that faction. There are millions of Christian Americans who agree with all or most of the policies supported by the Christian Coalition, but they strongly and rightly resist the notion that that is a test of whether or not they are Christians ["The Electoral Uses and Abuses of Religion," *First Things* 28 (December 1992), 5-7].

These essentially theological concerns have not been assuaged by the Christian Coalition's decision, in the aftermath of the 1992 election, to broaden its agenda (see

David S. Broder, "Christian Coalition, Shifting Tactics, to Lobby Against Clinton Budget," *Washington Post,* July 18, 1993). Nor are these concerns met by the *tu quoque* rejoinder that the Religious Left, as embodied in the "JustLife" voter guides, does the same thing.

16. Some would argue against the notion of "accommodation" here, but I think they would be mistaken. As a matter of social-ethical conviction as well as democratic conviction, I believe that the state ought to leave open a relatively wide space for personal behavior, including personal behavior that I find morally offensive. The boundaries of that private space are legitimate subjects of debate. But the alternative to democratic "accommodation" is a confessional state established according to one faction's understanding of the demands of Christian morals: and I take it that most thoughtful people on the Religious Right are opposed to that, on specifically religious grounds.

17. Irving Kristol, "The Coming Conservative Century," *Wall Street Journal,* February 1, 1993; this appears in adapted form as the foreword to this volume.

Response by RICHARD LAND

1. Carl F. H. Henry, *God, Revelation and Authority* (Waco: Word, 1976), vol. 2, 104-23.

2. Cf. Jonathan Edwards, "On the Insufficiency of Reason as a Substitute for Revelation," in *The Works of Jonathan Edwards* (Edinburgh: Banner of Truth Trust, 1974 reprint).

3. George Barna, *What Americans Believe: The Barna Report* (Ventura, CA: Regal Books, 1991), 83-85.

4. Charles W. Colson, *The Enduring Revolution* (Washington, D.C.: The Wilberforce Forum, 1993), 4-9.

5. Richard John Neuhaus, "A New Order of Religious Freedom," *First Things* 20 (February 1992), 15.

6. "Congress shall make no law respecting an establishment of religion, or prohibiting the free exercise thereof."

7. Charles W. Colson, "Reading the Pagan Mind," *Christianity Today,* November 9, 1992, 112, citing a Gallup Poll.

8. Ibid.

9. Colson, *The Enduring Revolution,* 9-10.

Index of Names

DATE DUE